Grades K–1

Teaching by Design in Elementary Mathematics

Jennifer Stepanek | Melinda Leong

Linda Griffin | Lisa Lavelle

A Joint Publication

CORWIN
A SAGE Company

education
northwest

For information:

 Corwin
A SAGE Company
2455 Teller Road
Thousand Oaks, California 91320
(800) 233-9936
Fax: (800) 417-2466
www.corwin.com

SAGE India Pvt. Ltd.
B 1/I 1 Mohan Cooperative Industrial Area
Mathura Road, New Delhi 110 044
India

SAGE Ltd.
1 Oliver's Yard
55 City Road
London EC1Y 1SP
United Kingdom

SAGE Asia-Pacific Pte. Ltd.
33 Pekin Street #02-01
Far East Square
Singapore 048763

Printed in the United States of America.

Library of Congress Cataloging-in-Publication Data

Teaching by design in elementary mathematics, grades K–1 / Jennifer Stepanek . . . [et al].
    p. cm.
"A Joint Publication with Education Northwest."
Includes bibliographical references and index.
ISBN 978-1-4129-8704-2 (pbk.)

    1. Mathematics—Study and teaching (Elementary) 2. Teaching teams. I. Stepanek, Jennifer (Jennifer Lynn) II. Education Northwest (U.S.) III. Title.

QA135.6.T365 2011
372.7—dc22   2010038716

This book is printed on acid-free paper.

10   11   12   13   14   10 9   8   7   6   5   4   3   2   1

Acquisitions Editor:	Dan Alpert
Associate Editor:	Megan Bedell
Editorial Assistant:	Sarah Bartlett
Production Editor:	Cassandra Margaret Seibel
Copy Editor:	Gretchen Treadwell
Typesetter:	C&M Digitals (P) Ltd.
Proofreader:	Susan Schon
Indexer:	Jean Casalegno
Cover Designer:	Michael Dubowe
Permissions Editor:	Karen Ehrmann

Teaching
by
Design
in
Elementary
Mathematics

Contents

Acknowledgments

We were privileged to have the support of many contributors throughout the process of developing this book.

In particular, we would like to thank the teachers at Riverview Elementary School—Leslie Carroll, Marla Ernst, Kristy Geddes, Beth Moore, Raylene Sell, Sheri Wardlaw—and Green Acres Elementary School—Jana Horne, Evan Kay, Chelsea Lewis, Danae Standfield, Julie Verbeck, and Leah Yeager—in Lebanon, Oregon. Their enthusiasm, dedication, and willingness to try new things were instrumental in creating the *Teaching by Design* materials. We are especially grateful to Marla Ernst and Lebanon Community Schools for supporting and facilitating our work with this terrific group of people.

We would also like to thank our colleagues for their careful review of the manuscript and their thoughtful feedback and suggestions. Joe Ediger, Bill Jackson, Mark Mitchell, Julie Peck, Neil Portnoy, and Nanci Schneider were very generous with their time and expertise. Liza Finkel, Claire Gates, and Kit Peixotto also reviewed early drafts and provided indispensible support to the writing team.

About the Authors

Jennifer Stepanek is a writer, editor, and researcher with Education Northwest in Portland, Oregon. She is the lead author of *Leading Lesson Study: A Practical Guide for Teachers and Facilitators* (2007), published by Corwin Press. She has worked with lesson study teams at a variety of sites in the Northwest to explore how teachers in the United States are adapting the Japanese model to fit their contexts and needs. She has written and edited a number of articles on lesson study and is also the coauthor of *An Invitation to Lesson Study*, an electronic resource designed to help facilitators and other professional development providers introduce lesson study to others. Her previous projects include serving as the editor of *Northwest Teacher*, a math and science journal; and writing publications for the *It's Just Good Teaching* series, research-based monographs on mathematics and science teaching.

Melinda Leong has served as a Senior Program Advisor in the Mathematics Education Unit at Education Northwest since 2001, providing leadership in designing effective professional development in mathematics learning, teaching, and assessment. Before joining Education Northwest, she worked with the New York City Board of Education in District 2 as a teacher and director for 11 years at the K–8 level. She was the founder and director of the Manhattan Academy of Technology in New York, a middle school focused on integrating technology into a three-year comprehensive and rigorous academic program. She holds a BA in education and American studies from Tufts University, an MA in elementary education from Hunter College at the City University of New York, an MA in administration and supervision from City College at the City University of New York, and a graduate certificate in middle school mathematics from Portland State University.

Linda Griffin is an Assistant Professor in the Graduate School of Education and Counseling at Lewis & Clark College in Portland, Oregon where she serves as the director of the Early MAT Early Childhood/Elementary Program. From 2004 to 2010, she served as the director of the Mathematics Education Unit at Education Northwest. Her professional background includes fourteen years as a middle and high school mathematics teacher, as well as eight years working on National Science Foundation grant projects focused on teacher enhancement, gender equity, and parent involvement in the area of mathematics. She has extensive experience conducting staff development and presenting workshops at regional and national conferences and has taught university courses in mathematics, including mathematics content courses for preservice elementary teachers. She holds a BA in mathematics from the University of California at Davis, an MA in teaching and teacher education from the University of Arizona, and an EdD in educational leadership from Northern Arizona University.

 **Lisa Lavelle** is Senior Curriculum Specialist in Mathematics at American Institutes for Research (AIR) where she is primarily involved in curriculum design and professional development for teachers. She also teaches math methods at Portland State University as an adjunct instructor. Prior to joining AIR, she served as Senior Program Advisor in the Mathematics Education Unit at Education Northwest, taught mathematics in both middle school and high school, served as a support teacher for elementary school mathematics, and worked with both preservice and inservice teachers in professional development. She earned her BA in psychology with emphasis in computer science from Yale University and at the same time completed the Teacher Preparation Program in secondary mathematics at Yale. She went on to earn her MA in professional studies, middle school mathematics, from George Washington University.

Introduction

What Is *Teaching by Design?*

Teaching by Design in Elementary Mathematics is a series of professional development guides that helps teachers create and share knowledge for teaching mathematics. This guide is one of three volumes in a set that focuses on topics within number and operations from kindergarten through Grade 5. Each volume in the series is organized in 14 professional development sessions in which teams of teachers learn, share, and plan together in a structured collaborative environment.

Through participation in the carefully sequenced sessions in each guide, teachers build the specialized understanding of mathematics and pedagogy that supports effective instruction. The culmination of this professional learning process is the development of a *prototype lesson*, a mathematics lesson collaboratively designed by the team. In teaching this prototype lesson in one or more teachers' classrooms, the team can investigate its impact on student learning. The cycle of investigating, planning, teaching, observing, debriefing, and revising a lesson together contributes to a climate of continuous professional learning.

Expected Outcomes for Teaching by Design in Elementary Mathematics

1. Teachers will deepen their content knowledge of important mathematical concepts for the grade level they teach.
2. Teachers will increase their understanding of how students learn these mathematical ideas.
3. Teachers will use their knowledge to develop effective lessons and improve instruction.
4. Teachers will enhance their collaboration skills.

Mathematical Content Topics

Several sources were consulted to identify the mathematical focus for each volume in the *Teaching by Design* series. The content is aligned with the topics in number and operations identified by the National Council of Teachers of Mathematics (NCTM) in *Curriculum Focal Points for Prekindergarten Through Grade 8 Mathematics* (2006). The focal points help teachers to hone in on the most important topics, make connections between topics, and to provide students with an integrated understanding of mathematics. The mathematical content of *Teaching by Design* also matches content topics in number and operations found in the *Common Core State Standards* (National Governors Association Center for Best Practices, & Council of Chief State School Officers, 2010).

Number and operations was selected as the content area for these materials because it is the cornerstone of mathematics education in Grades K–5. All mathematics is grounded in number, including algebra, geometry, measurement, and statistics (NCTM, 2000). This area of the curriculum is often considered to be the most simple and straightforward because it is the mathematics with which young children start their education. But learning about number and operations is in fact a complex process that has been a primary area of research in mathematics education (Fuson, 2003; Kilpatrick, Swafford, & Findell, 2001).

Model of Professional Development

One of the strengths of the *Teaching by Design in Elementary Mathematics* process is its alignment with the characteristics of effective professional development for teachers (Borasi & Fonzi, 2002; Corcoran, 1995; Garet, Porter, Desimone, Birman, & Yoon, 2001; Hawley & Valli, 1999; Darling-Hammond, Wei, Andree, Richardson, & Orphanos, 2009; Wilson & Berne, 1999). Specifically, effective learning experiences for teachers include the following characteristics:

- Opportunities for collaboration
- Ongoing activities
- Focus on content
- Teacher-driven and classroom-based methods
- Active and hands-on activities
- Focus on student learning

The *Teaching by Design* approach has been developed with these characteristics in mind to preserve this connection to high-quality professional development.

Teachers who are implementing any model for collaborative professional development can use *Teaching by Design*. Figure 1 provides a list describing some of these models and their features. Teacher teams that have already established one of these models for ongoing, job-embedded professional development will find that *Teaching by Design* is easily implemented within any of these models.

Teachers familiar with lesson study will recognize many of its features in the *Teaching by Design* materials (Fernandez & Chokshi, 2002; Lewis, 2002; Stigler & Hiebert, 1999; Yoshida, 1999). The sessions in each volume have been structured to provide support for the powerful practices of lesson study within any collaborative professional development model. Some of the practices from lesson study that will be evident in the *Teaching by Design* volumes include the following activities:

- Analyzing teaching materials
- Focusing on important content
- Establishing precise and connected lesson goals
- Developing well-planned lessons
- Observing student learning
- Analyzing student understanding

Teacher teams that have not previously engaged in one of these professional development models will still be able to successfully implement *Teaching by Design*. An informal group of grade-level teaching partners can use the materials provided as a way to take a first step toward establishing one of these professional development models. The resources section includes some recommended readings about each model that will assist groups that want to know more about them.

Figure 1   Models of Professional Development

Critical friends groups (CFG)	A group of teachers work together to examine and change their classroom practice guided by established group processes and protocols.
	Typical features: • A CFG coach guides the teachers' work. • The team uses CFG protocols to structure conversations about curriculum, student work, or relevant readings.
Lesson study	Teachers collaborate to develop a lesson plan, teach and observe the lesson to collect data on student learning, and use their observations to refine their lesson.
	Typical features: • Lesson study teams are self-directed and democratic, but may work with a facilitator and outside advisors. • The team has established protocols for designing, observing, debriefing, and revising collaboratively designed lessons.
Mathematics coaching	A specialist works with teachers one-on-one to examine and improve classroom practice and to improve pedagogical content knowledge.
	Typical features: • The mathematics coach works with individual teachers or grade-level teams of teachers. • The coach and teachers commonly observe each other teaching a lesson or coteach lessons.
Professional learning teams	Small groups of teachers work together to improve instruction and student learning.
	Typical features: • Members of the group share leadership of the group. • The team engages in reading and discussion on topics of professional interest to the group.

Collaborating to Design a Prototype Lesson

Why Design?

The term *design* generally refers to the creation of a product in an artistic or highly skilled manner, and it is usually associated with the applied arts, engineering, and architecture. In these contexts, good design means that the product fits the needs of the people who will use it and the context in which it will be used.

One of the more specific definitions of design is the process of preparing a detailed and deliberate plan for accomplishing something (Merriam-Webster, 1993). This definition is the essence of *Teaching by Design*. It is a way to describe teachers' work that focuses on planning well-designed lessons that fit the needs of their students.

Some of the general practices of design have parallels with teaching, and include the following practices:

• Identifying and framing problems and needs
• Working collaboratively

- Gathering and analyzing information
- Determining performance criteria for successful solutions
- Generating alternative solutions and building prototypes
- Evaluating and selecting appropriate solutions
- Implementing choices
- Evaluating outcomes

> "A teacher ideally conceived is a designer who helps learners design themselves."
>
> —David Perkins, *Knowledge as Design*

When architects or mechanical designers work on a project, they almost always collaborate with other professionals. Designing a building, a computer, or a refrigerator is complicated work and requires the best thinking of a team of experts. Similarly, well-designed lessons are often the product of several teachers working together to think deeply about the goals and strategize the best ways to help students achieve them.

In Sessions 2 through 11 of *Teaching by Design*, you will discuss and explore aspects of mathematics teaching and learning that will prepare you for Session 12, in which you will work together as a design team to develop a well-planned lesson. After the lesson has been taught in one or more classes, in Sessions 13 and 14 you will discuss the lesson results, then revise and improve the lesson. While the focus is on a single lesson designed by the group, the learning gained from the collaborative process will influence the many other lessons you plan individually.

Why Prototype Lessons?

In product design, a prototype is the original form of the product that serves as the basis or standard for other versions of that product. Through the *Teaching by Design* process, teachers will collaborate to design a *prototype* lesson. This lesson is the context through which teachers explore their ideas and questions about how students learn challenging mathematical concepts. As they design the prototype lesson together, teachers explore how to sequence learning experiences that engage students with important mathematics while strengthening students' problem-solving abilities. For designers, the implementation of a prototype provides information to enhance future products. Likewise, the implementation of the prototype lesson provides teaching teams with insights about teaching and learning that can be applied to the development and delivery of future lessons.

The prototype lesson provides an opportunity to incorporate the mathematical and pedagogical knowledge teachers have gained through the *Teaching by Design* sequence. The resulting lesson plan is more detailed than a typical lesson plan and represents teachers' collective ideas about helping students understand important mathematical ideas. In addition to laying out the learning activities and the sequence of instruction, the plan for the prototype lesson includes background information about the instructional decisions that have been made, goals for student learning, carefully worded questions and prompts, anticipated student responses and teacher supports, and points of evaluation. Including all these elements in the lesson plan facilitates the observation, debriefing, and revision of the lesson. It also serves as a record of the professional learning for this team while they are engaged in these professional development sessions.

The prototype lesson offers teachers a perfect opportunity to apply their knowledge and understanding of the following areas:

- *Mathematics content,* including their understanding of how the mathematical concepts are interconnected
- *Students' prior knowledge,* including what students have learned in previous lessons and what they have learned in prior grade levels or through experiences outside the classroom
- *Learning progressions,* including ideas of how students develop increasingly sophisticated strategies, big ideas, and models

Overview of the Sessions

The materials are organized into a series of 14 work sessions, each approximately 90 minutes long.

Session 1	Getting Started
Session 2	Learning Landscape
Session 3	Counting and Number Concepts
Session 4	Comparing and Ordering Numbers
Session 5	Addition and Subtraction Word Problems (Part 1)
Session 6	Addition and Subtraction Word Problems (Part 2)
Session 7	Children's Strategies: Direct Modeling
Session 8	Children's Strategies: Counting Strategies
Session 9	Children's Strategies: Numerical Reasoning
Session 10	Children's Strategies: Numerical Reasoning Using 10
Session 11	Mathematical Models Supporting Numerical Reasoning
Session 12	Designing the Prototype Lesson
Session 13	Discussing Results
Session 14	Reflecting On and Revising the Prototype Lesson

Sessions 1 and 2 establish a context for the work. In Session 1, teams will establish group norms and explore design principles. In Session 2, teachers will begin to develop components of a learning landscape for number and operations in kindergarten and first grade.

Sessions 3 through 11 focus on how children learn specific mathematical topics. The activities include opportunities to do mathematics problems, to examine how students learn, and to analyze and discuss student work. Some of the sessions include activities that focus on how the ideas from that session can be used to inform instruction.

Between sessions, teachers will engage in two types of activities. Student Connections activities are opportunities for teachers to observe student learning and collect student work. Investigating Instructional Materials activities are opportunities to analyze teaching resources. These activities are integral to subsequent sessions because they help illustrate important mathematical and pedagogical ideas and allow teachers to apply their learning to their practice.

During Session 11, the team begins work on the prototype lesson. The process of designing the lesson may take more than one meeting to complete. When the lesson is ready, one or more team members implement the lesson with their students. Session 13 should occur after the teaching of the lesson and is structured to provide teachers with an opportunity to discuss what happened and to analyze evidence of student learning. Depending on how many teachers implement the lesson, some teams will need additional time for this discussion. Session 14 gives teachers the opportunity to revise the lesson, reflect on the professional development process, and identify next steps.

Many times throughout *Teaching by Design*, you will be directed to write in your journal. It will be helpful to organize your journal into three sections: (1) Activities, (2) Student Connections, and (3) Lesson Design Notes. We suggest using either a binder with tabs or a composition book or spiral notebook with tabbed sections in which you take notes and staple handouts.

Facilitating

Each of the sessions is designed to be facilitated by one person. The facilitator can be a coach or team leader, or the facilitation role can rotate within the group. When team members take turns serving in this role, all of the teachers receive an opportunity to develop their leadership skills. In either case, the facilitator should take responsibility for previewing the session content and making sure that all the materials are prepared. During the session, the facilitator should also serve as the timekeeper and maintain the pace of the session.

Each session includes Facilitator Notes, outlining the specific responsibilities for that session. The notes include additional information the facilitator can use to support the work of the team. One of the key responsibilities during facilitation is helping to maintain the group norms that the team identifies in the first session. It is usually helpful for the team to revisit the list of group norms periodically to make sure they are adhering to the norms and to identify any additions or modifications to the list.

Another key responsibility for the facilitator is listening actively to the group's conversations throughout the session. The facilitator will help monitor the discussions and activities to ensure that all team members have an opportunity to participate, share their knowledge, and learn. The facilitator can also help get the discussions started with an initial observation or question if there is a lag in the conversation.

If a leader or coach will serve as the facilitator, keep in mind that the team is intended to be self-directed. All members of the team are responsible for making decisions, contributing equally to the work, and supporting their colleagues' professional learning. The resources listed at the end of this section provide for more information on the skills and responsibilities of facilitators in different types of professional learning teams.

Finding Time for Collaboration

Teaching by Design in Elementary Mathematics is intended to guide teams of teachers through a process of collaborative investigation that will deepen their knowledge for teaching mathematics. To engage in *Teaching by Design* sessions, teachers will need time to meet together. Ideally, each group will meet regularly and frequently. Having weekly or biweekly meetings keeps the momentum going while also allowing time for collecting student data between the sessions.

When opportunities for teacher collaboration are a regular part of the school schedule, finding time should not be an issue. However, even if collaboration time is not part of the existing schedule, teams can find other ways to meet. For example, team meetings can be held outside regular school hours before or after school. Teams may find that they have occasional opportunities to work for extended sessions on early-release days or on days scheduled for professional development. If this is the case, groups can complete more than one 90-minute session in that setting and collect student data to share at a subsequent meeting.

There are a number of excellent resources that specifically address the issues associated with finding time within the school schedule for school-based professional development and teacher collaboration time. Figure 2 illustrates the strategies schools have used to create more time for teachers to work together.

Figure 2 Strategies for Creating Time for Collaboration

Adjusting the School Schedule
Early Release/Late Start Four days a week, the school schedule is extended by several minutes. One day a week, students come to school one hour late or go home one hour early. A variation on this schedule is to have teachers come to school 30 minutes early, with students arriving 30 minutes late; a similar strategy can also be used at the end of the day. (An early release/late start schedule does not have to be used on a weekly basis but can be spread out over the course of several weeks.)
Professional Development Days The daily school schedule is extended by several minutes in order to release students for a full day once a month or every six weeks.
Prep Time Teachers in each grade level or each department have a common prep time that can be used weekly (or as needed) to work together.
Covering Classes
Specialist Days Each day of the week, students from one grade level spend most of the day with specialists, in the computer lab, and in the library.
Service Learning For one half-day each week, students spend their time conducting service learning or community projects.
Paraprofessionals/Administrators/Parents/Volunteers Teachers' classes are taken over for one hour each week.
Teaming Teacher teams pair up and take each other's classes for one hour each week. For example, each second-grade teacher takes one class of first graders so that the first-grade teachers can meet together.
Substitute Teachers Substitutes are hired to rotate through the classes one day every other week.
Reallocating Existing Time
Staff Meetings Weekly staff meetings are cut back to once or twice a month and replaced with grade-level or department meetings.
Adjusting Planning Time Teachers' daily planning time is used for collaborative work one day a week. The number of minutes that teachers are expected to stay after school can be cut back by 10 minutes on four days during the week in order to create an extra 40 minutes for meeting together on one afternoon.
Professional Development/Inservice Days Teachers are excused from staff development days to compensate for weekly meetings outside school hours.

References

Borasi, R., & Fonzi, J. (2002). *Professional development that supports school mathematics reform* (Vol. 3). Arlington, VA: National Science Foundation.

Corcoran, T. B. (1995). *Helping teachers teach well: Transforming professional development* (CPRE Policy Brief No. RB–16). New Brunswick, NJ: Rutgers, State University of New Jersey, Consortium for Policy Research in Education.

Darling-Hammond, L., Wei, R. C., Andree, A., Richardson, N., & Orphanos, S. (2009). *Professional learning in the learning profession: A status report on teacher development in the United States and abroad.* Oxford, OH: National Staff Development Council.

Fernandez, C., & Chokshi, S. (2002). A practical guide to translating lesson study for a U.S. setting. *Phi Delta Kappan, 84*(2), 128–134.

Fuson, K. C. (2003). Developing mathematical power in whole number operations. In J. Kilpatrick, W. G. Martin, & D. Schifter (Eds.), *A research companion to Principles and Standards for School Mathematics* (pp. 68–94). Reston, VA: National Council of Teachers of Mathematics.

Garet, M. S., Porter, A. C., Desimone, L., Birman, B. F., & Yoon, K. S. (2001). What makes professional development effective? Results from a national sample of teachers. *American Educational Research Journal, 38*(4), 915–945.

Hawley, W. D., & Valli, L. (1999). The essentials of effective professional development: A new consensus. In L. Darling-Hammond & G. Sykes (Eds.), *Teaching as the learning profession: Handbook of policy and practice* (pp. 127–150). San Francisco: Jossey-Bass.

Kilpatrick, J., Swafford, J., & Findell, B. (Eds.). (2001). *Adding it up: Helping children learn mathematics.* Washington, DC: National Academies Press.

Lewis, C. (2002). *Lesson study: A handbook of teacher-led instructional change.* Philadelphia: Research for Better Schools.

Merriam-Webster's collegiate dictionary (10th ed.). (1993). Springfield, MA: Merriam-Webster.

National Council of Teachers of Mathematics (2000). *Principles and standards for school mathematics.* Arlington, VA: Author.

National Council of Teachers of Mathematics. (2006). *Curriculum focal points for prekindergarten through grade 8 mathematics: A quest for coherence.* Reston, VA: Author.

National Governors Association Center for Best Practices, & Council of Chief State School Officers. (2010). *Common Core State Standards: Mathematics.* Retrieved from http://www.corestandards.org/the-standards/mathematics/

Stigler, J. W., & Hiebert, J. (1999). *The teaching gap: Best ideas from the world's teachers for improving education in the classroom.* New York: Free Press.

Wilson, S. M., & Berne, J. (1999). Teacher learning and the acquisition of professional knowledge: An examination of research on contemporary professional development. In A. Iran-Nejad & P. D. Pearson (Eds.), *Review of research in education* (Vol. 24, pp. 173–209). Washington, DC: American Educational Research Association.

Yoshida, M. (1999, April). *Lesson study [jugyokenkyu] in elementary school mathematics in Japan: A case study.* Paper presented at the annual meeting of the American Educational Research Association, Montreal, Canada.

Additional Resources

Critical Friends Groups

National School Reform Faculty
http://www.nsrfharmony.org/faq.html#1

Coalition of Essential Schools Northwest
http://www.cesnorthwest.org/cfg.php

Allen, D., & Blythe, T. (2004). *A facilitator's book of questions: Resources for looking together at student and teacher work.* New York: Teachers College Press.

Lesson Study

Lesson Study Group at Mills College
http://www.lessonresearch.net/

Lesson Study Northwest Regional Educational Laboratory, Center for Classroom Teaching and Learning
http://educationnorthwest.org/service/235

Lewis, C. (2002). *Lesson study: A handbook of teacher-led instructional change.* Philadelphia: Research for Better Schools.

Stepanek, J., Appel, G., Leong, M., Mangan, M. T., & Mitchell, M. (2007). *Leading lesson study: A practical guide for teachers and facilitators.* Thousand Oaks, CA: Corwin.

Mathematics Coaches

Examining the Role of a Math Content Coach Eye on Education
http://www.eyeoneducation.com/Excerpts/7093-8%20Math%20Coaching%20Chapter%201.pdf

Pedagogical Content Coaching Silicon Valley Mathematics Initiative
http://www.noycefdn.org/documents/math/pedagogicalcontentcoaching.pdf

West, L., & Staub, F. C. (2003). *Content-focused coaching: Transforming mathematics lessons.* Portsmouth, NH: Heinemann.

Professional Learning Teams

Hord, S. M. (1997). Professional Learning Communities: What Are They and Why Are They Important? *Issues . . . About Change, 6*(1). Retrieved from www.sedl.org/change/issues/issues61.html

Sather, S. E. (2005). *Improving instruction through professional learning teams: A guide for school leaders.* Portland, OR: Northwest Regional Educational Laboratory. Retrieved from http://educationnorthwest.org/catalog/improving-instruction-through-professional-learning-teams-guide-school-leaders

Professional Learning Teams (PLTs) to Improve Student Achievement Education Northwest http://educationnorthwest.org/service/295

Session 1
Getting Started

What can we do to create the conditions that enhance professional learning?

Description

The need for collaborative professional learning is well established, but forming a group is only the first step. Collaboration can be challenging, so laying the groundwork for an effective and worthwhile experience is key. In this session, you will initiate *Teaching by Design* by establishing a common understanding of the process, group norms, and shared goals.

Key Ideas

- Some of the general practices of design have parallels with teaching.
- Well-designed lessons are often the product of several teachers working together to think deeply about their goals and strategize the best ways to help students achieve them.
- Establishing group norms helps a team to operate productively.
- Groups function best when they have a common understanding of their goals and outcomes.

Outline of Activities

- 1.1 What is *Teaching by Design?*   (15 minutes)
- 1.2 Number Window   (25 minutes)
- 1.3 *Teaching by Design* Themes   (20 minutes)
- 1.4 Setting Group Norms   (15 minutes)
- 1.5 Group Outcomes and Personal Goals   (10 minutes)
- 1.6 Before the Next Session   (5 minutes)

What to Bring

- A journal (see the description and suggestions in the Introduction) and writing instruments (bring these to every session)

To Complete Before Session 2

- Lesson Design Notes (Handout 1.3)

Facilitator Notes   Session 1

Getting Started

Before the session, please review the more detailed facilitator guidelines in the Introduction. As the facilitator, it is generally your job to keep the conversation flowing and watch the clock. Use your judgment to decide when it's appropriate to extend a session for good conversation or when it's time to move on to the next activity. Remember to keep the group norms posted and revise them, as a group, as necessary.

Before the Session

- Make copies of the following handouts for each team member:
    - ☐ 1.1 Design Practices
    - ☐ 1.2 Number Window
    - ☐ 1.3 Lesson Design Notes
- Gather the following materials to be used in this session:
    - ☐ Chart paper
    - ☐ Markers
    - ☐ Counters
- Remind team members to bring the following items:
    - ☐ Journal (see the description and suggestions in the Introduction)
    - ☐ Writing instruments

During the Session

- Activity 1.1: facilitate partnering, if necessary.
- Activity 1.2: facilitate partnering, if necessary.
- Activity 1.4: lead development of group norms, and serve as recorder.

After the Session

- Pass the group norms on to the next facilitator.

Activity 1.1 What is *Teaching by Design?*

15 minutes   Handout 1.1 Design Practices

Teaching by Design in Elementary Mathematics is a guide for professional development that helps teachers improve their knowledge for teaching mathematics. By engaging in the *Teaching by Design* process as a team, you will build a better understanding of mathematics and student learning.

We purposefully chose to link the terms *teaching* and *design* to describe this professional development experience. As noted in the Introduction, the term *design* is often associated with the applied arts, engineering, and architecture to describe the creation of a product in an artistic or highly skilled manner. Design in these contexts involves establishing goodness of fit between a product, the people who will use it, and the context in which it will be used. *Teaching by Design* is a way to describe teachers' work that focuses on planning deliberate and purposeful lessons that fit the needs of their students.

Discuss the following list of design practices with a partner. Consider how these practices might be applied to planning and teaching a lesson. Handout 1.1 provides this list in a table that can be used to record your ideas.

- Identifying and framing problems and needs
- Working collaboratively
- Gathering and analyzing information
- Determining performance criteria for successful solutions
- Generating alternative solutions and building prototypes
- Evaluating and selecting appropriate solutions
- Implementing choices
- Evaluating outcomes

Share what you and your partner listed with the whole group. In what ways does teaching include some of these design principles? Which ones have the strongest parallels to lesson design?

Activity 1.2 Number Window

25 minutes   Handout 1.2 Number Window
                                                                               Counters

Throughout the *Teaching by Design* experience, you will have the chance to engage in student activities that can be used in your classroom. Participating in these activities and analyzing their instructional benefits is intended to stimulate discussion of a range of teaching and learning issues.

Place up to eight counters in each quadrant of your window on Handout 1.2. Each quadrant may contain zero to eight counters. Two quadrants may (but don't have to) contain the same number of counters.

Find the total number of counters in each row and column and **write** the four sums in the spaces provided. When you are finished, remove the counters.

Trade your completed window with a partner. Use the sums to recreate the counters in each quadrant of the window. When you are finished, remove the counters.

Trade with a third team member. Use the sums to recreate the counters in each quadrant of the window.

Discuss the following questions:

- What thinking process did you use to solve your partners' puzzles?

- What observations or generalizations can you make about window arrangements?

- Is this mathematical activity similar to any activities you use in your classroom? Describe the related activities.

- Is this mathematical activity appropriate for your students? If not, what adaptations could you make so it would be appropriate for your students?

Activity 1.3 *Teaching by Design* Themes

20 minutes   Handout 1.3 Lesson Design Notes

As you and your team engage in the *Teaching by Design* sessions, you will discuss and explore many aspects of mathematics teaching and learning that will prepare you to work together to collaboratively plan a mathematics lesson. Each session will include opportunities for you to reflect on three key themes related to teaching and learning.

Read the following quotation about teaching and think about how it relates to your own experiences.

> To teach math, you need to know three things. You need to know where you are now (in terms of the knowledge children in your classroom have available to build upon). You need to know where you want to go (in terms of the knowledge you want all children in your classroom to acquire during the school year). Finally, you need to know what is the best way to get there (in terms of the learning opportunities you will provide to enable all children in your class to achieve your stated objectives). Although this sounds simple, each of these points is just the tip of an iceberg. Each raises a question (e.g., Where are we now?) that I have come to believe is crucial for the design of effective mathematics instruction. Each also points to a body of knowledge (the iceberg) to which teachers must have access in order to answer that question . . .
>
> By asking this set of questions every time I sat down to design a math lesson for young children, I was able to push my thinking further and, over time, construct better answers and better lessons. If each math teacher asks this set of questions on a regular basis, each will be able to construct his or her own set of answers for the questions, enrich our knowledge base, and improve mathematics teaching and learning for at least one group of children.
>
> Sharon Griffin, *How Students Learn* (2005, p. 257–258)

Discuss the three questions described in the quotation and apply them to your classroom.

Record your ideas on Handout 1.3 Lesson Design Notes.

- Where are you now?
  - What knowledge do your students currently have about number and operations? What are they able to do and what do they understand?
  - Which of your students have greater needs than others? Describe the range of understanding that your students are currently demonstrating.
  - How can you find out more about each student's mathematical understanding?

- Where do you want to go?
  - What are your long-term goals for students?
  - What do you want your students to know and understand by the end of kindergarten or first grade?
  - What attitudes and beliefs about mathematics do you want your students to develop?

- What is the best way to get there?
  - What routines do you use that support student learning?
  - How do you identify and choose instructional approaches?
  - How do you use your knowledge of your students' current levels of understanding to inform your instructional decisions?
  - How do you scaffold your lessons to provide support for students who need extra help and challenge those students who finish quickly?

You will continue to add new ideas and questions to the Lesson Design Notes in future sessions. Staple or tape Handout 1.3 into your journal and set up a section with room for additional notes. This will help you capture all of your lesson design ideas in one place.

Activity 1.4 Setting Group Norms

15 minutes

Collaboration can be challenging at times, even in a group of willing and committed partners. Laying the groundwork for an effective and worthwhile experience is key to managing any bumps in the road.

Consider the following questions and **write** your answers in your journal. Treat this like a brainstorming activity. Try to get as many ideas on paper as possible.

- What expectations do you have for how the group will work together?
- What conditions get in the way of learning and sharing?
- What group features help you to feel a sense of belonging and support?

Before you share your list with the group and develop group norms, read the following ideas about effective group processes (Bray, Lee, Smith, & Yorks, 2000; Collay, Dunlap, Enloe, & Gagnon, 1998; Dufour & Eaker, 1998; Preskill & Torres, 1999). Reading this list might prompt new ideas that you would like to add to your journal, so feel free to add to or edit your list based on the following ideas.

- *Groups work well when communication is open and honest.* Team members must feel that they are able to share their ideas and opinions without inspiring defensiveness or reprisals. It will be difficult for members to learn from each other if they cannot be honest. Although the ability to share their views openly and honestly is important, members will be unlikely to do so if they fear their contributions will be ignored or belittled. The balance between honesty and trust may not be easy to establish and maintain at first, but it is crucial to the team's work.

- *Groups work well when members both challenge and support each other.* Team members do this by asking questions, building on each other's ideas, and respectfully disagreeing. They are expected to ask for clarification, explain their reasoning, and provide evidence to back up their assertions.

- *Groups work well when methods for resolving conflict are established and agreed upon.* No team should begin its work with the assumption that it will be easy to work together. Members must agree to listen and focus on the problem rather than on the people involved, give the process adequate time, and try to see the issue from another person's perspective.

- *Groups work well when mistakes are viewed as opportunities.* It is difficult to try new things or to take risks if you fear the consequences. It may be helpful to keep in mind that mistakes are fruitful sources of learning—so, in many ways, the more the better.

- *Groups work well when all members are held accountable for their actions.* Part of engaging in collaborative learning is making a commitment to the other team members. All must agree to fulfill their specific responsibilities, to share the work as equally as possible, and to support each other and maintain productive and respectful interactions.

Share your list with the group. The facilitator will keep a running list on chart paper as each person takes turns sharing. Keep going around the room until all ideas are represented on the paper. **Discuss** and **refine** the list so that it reflects the consensus of the group.

Maintaining Group Norms

This list of group norms will serve as a charter for your team. The final list should be posted each time the group meets or it can be transferred to a handout that group members keep in their journals.

Remember that establishing group norms is only the first step. You will need to continually monitor your own participation and hold your colleagues to the norms. Do not wait until a problem arises to review the list and reflect on your collaborative practices.

Activity 1.5 Group Outcomes and Personal Goals

10 minutes

Teaching by Design in Elementary Mathematics has the following expected outcomes.

> **Expected Outcomes for *Teaching by Design***
>
> 1. Teachers will deepen their content knowledge of important mathematical concepts for the grade level they teach.
> 2. Teachers will increase their understanding of how students learn these mathematical ideas.
> 3. Teachers will use their knowledge to develop effective lessons and improve instruction.
> 4. Teachers will enhance their collaboration skills.

Discuss what each outcome means to you. Do these outcomes match your own expectations for this professional development process? What additional goals do you have for the group?

Write your answers to some of the following questions in your journal:

- How do you expect this professional development process to impact your teaching?
- In what ways do you think this process will impact your relationships with your colleagues in this group?
- What personal goals do you have for your work with *Teaching by Design?*

Activity 1.6 Before the Next Session

5 minutes

Write additional questions and ideas on your Lesson Design Notes. As you work with your students between now and the next sessions, find out more about their mathematical understanding and add this data under "Where are you now?"

Read the Introduction to *Teaching by Design in Elementary Mathematics* if you have not done so already. This will give you a broader sense of the intent of this type of professional development as well as some tips for facilitating your time together. Consider how your personal goals are connected to the *Teaching by Design* process.

References and Resources

Bray, J. N., Lee, J., Smith, L. L., & Yorks, L. (2000). *Collaborative inquiry in practice: Action, reflection, and making meaning.* Thousand Oaks, CA: Sage.

Collay, M., Dunlap, D., Enloe, W., & Gagnon, G. W., Jr. (1998). *Learning circles: Creating conditions for professional development.* Thousand Oaks, CA: Corwin.

Dufour, R., & Eaker, R. (1998). *Professional learning communities at work: Best practices for enhancing student achievement.* Bloomington, IN: National Educational Service.

Griffin, S. (2005). Fostering the development of whole number sense: Teaching mathematics in the primary grades. In M. S. Donovan & J. D. Bransford (Eds.), *How students learn: Mathematics in the classroom* (pp. 257–308). Washington, DC: National Academies Press.

Preskill, H., & Torres, R. T. (1999). *Evaluative inquiry for learning in organizations.* New York: Doubleday.

Handout 1.1
Design Practices

Design Practices in Applied Arts, Engineering, and Architecture	Application of the Practice to Lesson Planning and Lesson Delivery
Identifying and framing problems and needs	
Working collaboratively	
Gathering and analyzing information	
Determining performance criteria for successful solutions	
Generating alternative solutions and building prototypes	
Evaluating and selecting appropriate solutions	
Implementing choices	
Evaluating outcomes	

Handout 1.2
Number Window

_____

_____

_____   _____

Handout 1.3
Lesson Design Notes

	Ideas and Questions
Where are you now?	
Where do you want to go?	
What is the best way to get there?	

Session 2

Learning Landscape

How can a learning landscape help teachers understand children's mathematical development?

Description

A learning landscape can function as a "map" of student learning. The landscape may include mathematical big ideas, strategies, and models. Learning does not follow a linear trajectory. Rather, students may move across the learning landscape in different ways as they develop understanding of mathematical concepts.

Key Ideas

- A learning landscape can function as a map of student learning for teachers.

- A learning landscape includes three domains: (1) strategies, (2) big ideas, and (3) mathematical models.

Outline of Activities

- 2.1 What Is a Learning Landscape?   (30 minutes)
- 2.2 Quick Peek Game   (25 minutes)
- 2.3 Components of a Learning Landscape   (25 minutes)
- 2.4 Before the Next Session   (5 minutes)
- 2.5 Lesson Design Notes   (5 minutes)

What to Bring

- Journal (and writing instruments)

To Complete Before Session 3

- Student Connections: Observing Counting Strategies (Handout 2.4)

Facilitator Notes   Session 2

Learning Landscape

If this is your first time facilitating the group, please refer to the more detailed facilitator guidelines in the Introduction. As the facilitator, it is generally your job to keep the conversation flowing and watch the clock. Use your judgment to decide when it's appropriate to extend a session for good conversation or when it's time to move on to the next activity. Remember to keep the group norms posted and revise them, as a group, as necessary.

Before the Session

- Make copies of the following handouts for each team member:
    - ☐ 2.1 Getting From Here to There
    - ☐ 2.2 Dot Card Patterns
    - ☐ 2.3 Components of a Learning Landscape
    - ☐ 2.4 Student Connections: Observing Counting Strategies

- Gather the following materials to be used in this session:
    - ☐ Group norms (from Activity 1.4)
    - ☐ Small paper plates (or ask each team member to bring a stack)
    - ☐ Markers (at least two colors)
    - ☐ Adhesive dots (at least two colors)

- Remind team members to bring the following items from previous sessions:
    - ☐ Journal (and writing instruments)

During the Session

- Post group norms, and revise as a group as necessary.

- Activity 2.2: facilitate partnering, if necessary.

After the Session

- Remind team members of homework, Handout 2.4 Student Connections: Observing Counting Strategies.

- Pass any team materials on to the next facilitator.

Activity 2.1 What Is a Learning Landscape?

30 minutes   Handout 2.1 Getting From Here to There

Can you think of a time when you were planning to drive somewhere and needed directions? Before the age of the Internet, most of us relied on maps to plot our routes and to find our way when we got lost. Now it is very common to use electronically generated sets of turn-by-turn directions to get from here to there. On websites like maps.yahoo.com, mapquest.com, and maps.google.com you can print out detailed directions for trips. You can even get real-time turn-by-turn directions by using a portable Global Positioning System (GPS) device in your car. Some might argue that these new navigation tools will eventually make paper maps obsolete.

Think about the kind of information you get when you use turn-by-turn directions compared to the kind of information you get from a printed map. What are the advantages and disadvantages of these two kinds of navigation tools? What do you gain or lose by choosing one navigation mode over the other?

Record your ideas on Handout 2.1.

Discuss how this analogy of navigation relates to teaching.

- In what ways is planning for teaching like planning for a trip?

- What kinds of documents or tools do you use that serve the function of maps or turn-by-turn directions?

- Do you ever feel "lost" when teaching? What do you do about it?

- Do you feel that all of your students are "on the same road" with you?

- Are there particular "landmarks" you watch for in student learning?

Reflect on two of your students, one who is very capable in mathematics and one who struggles with number concepts. **Write** in your journal about the differences between these two students.

- What qualities does the capable student have that the struggling student does not?

- What factors contribute to the success of one student and the challenges of the other?

- Would you say they have similar learning progressions?

- Are they progressing through their mathematical understanding in the same order but at different paces?

- What do you need to know about student learning to help the struggling student catch up with the capable student?

- What do you need to know about student learning in order to continue to challenge the capable student?

- Where is each student on the "travel plan" that you described?

As you may have concluded in your earlier discussion, a scope and sequence document or a textbook that you follow page-by-page could be thought of as a form of turn-by-turn directions for teaching. When you are guided in this way, you don't really have to look ahead; you just turn the page and do what it says. It provides an efficient route to get most students to the goal of learning mathematical concepts and procedures.

However, as with turn-by-turn directions, following a textbook sequence might not provide you with the big picture or map that you need to help *all* students reach the goal of mathematical understanding. As all teachers know, some children take "detours" in their learning or don't start at the point the textbook assumes. If teachers had a map that described how students typically progress in their mathematical understanding, they would have greater flexibility to "adjust the route" because they could plot many paths to get to the final goal. The big picture that lays out what is most important for students to learn and many routes that students might take to get there has thus been called a *landscape of learning.*

Read this quotation describing a landscape of learning.

Landscape of Learning is a metaphor chosen to characterize children's mathematical development. The metaphor of a landscape suggests a picture of a learning terrain in which students move in meandering or direct ways as they develop strategies and ideas about mathematical topics.

Along students' journeys there are moments of uncertainty, moments of potential shifts in understanding (crossroads), and moments where mathematical ideas or strategies are constructed (landmarks).

Knowledge of these moments gives teachers the capacity to better understand, document, and stretch students' thinking.

Maarten Dolk and Catherine Twomey Fosnot,
Fostering Children's Mathematical Development:
The Landscape of Learning (2006, p. vii)

Fosnot and Dolk emphasize that the landscape of learning is not sequential or linear—students follow their own paths as they move around the landscape. As a result, it cannot be used as a checklist of outcomes. This landscape is also fluid, rather than static: "As in any real journey, new landmarks can appear, and new paths, unchartered before, can be carved out. The landscape . . . is simply a representation of others' past journeys—it can inform teaching, but it can also be added to as teachers work with the young mathematicians in their classrooms" (Fosnot & Dolk, 2001, p. 163).

Discuss what this metaphor means to you. How does a landscape of learning relate to the comments you wrote in your journal about the ways planning for teaching is like planning for a trip?

Share what you wrote about your two students with the group. What similarities and differences do you notice in the group's responses? How do the quotes from Dolk and Fosnot and their metaphor of a landscape of learning relate to the variation in student learning that you recorded?

Activity 2.2 Quick Peek Game

25 minutes

Handout 2.2 Dot Card Patterns
About 20 paper plates
Adhesive dots in at least two colors (or markers in two colors)

This game can help teachers learn about students' number sense and fluency with quantities to 10.

Make a set of dot plates following the models on the dot plate handout. Each person in the group can make a few so that the group has a complete set. Place all the plates face down within easy reach of all group members.

Find a partner for the game.

Take turns turning over a plate and showing it to your partner. Reveal the plate for a slow count of 2 seconds, and then turn the plate back over. The other player says how many dots were visible on the plate and describes the arrangement of the dots. Return your plate to the central pile and choose another plate. Play for 5 to 8 minutes.

Discuss what made some numbers easier to identify than others.

- What visual clues did you rely on (e.g., triangular or square arrangements, two identical sets)?
- Is this mathematical activity similar to any activities you use in your classroom? Share related activities.
- Is this mathematical activity appropriate for your students? If not, what adaptations could you make to the activity for your students?

Both adults and children can identify small numbers of objects without counting. This process is called *subitizing*. We can also easily identify collections without counting when they are arranged in familiar patterns or when they can be seen as two smaller collections (for example, using two colors). Identifying quantities without having to count them can aid students in developing more sophisticated and efficient strategies for counting and learning number combinations. Practice with visual patterns and arrangements can help students move in this direction more quickly (Van de Walle, 2009).

Activity 2.3 Components of a Learning Landscape

25 minutes

Handout 2.3 Components of a Learning Landscape

In this activity, you will identify components of a learning landscape for mathematics based on your knowledge of student learning. The learning landscape in mathematics includes three domains: (1) strategies, (2) big ideas, and (3) mathematical models. *Strategies* are the methods that students use to solve problems or to make sense of a situation. *Big ideas* are the important mathematical concepts that form the basis for future learning. *Mathematical models* are physical, visual, and abstract ways to represent mathematical relationships and situations. In the following grey box, you will find some examples of components for each of these domains related to primary grades.

Learning Landscape: Domains and Components

Strategies are the methods that students use to solve problems or to make sense of a situation.

Examples

- Using physical objects to represent a situation
- Counting on or skip counting
- Using relationships between numbers to simplify a calculation

Big ideas are the important mathematical concepts that form the basis for future learning.

Examples

- A quantity can be separated into parts in various ways without changing the value.
- The order in which quantities are combined does not change the total (commutative property of addition).
- An action that is "done" then "undone" returns a quantity to its original value (inverse principle).

Mathematical models are physical, visual, and abstract ways to represent mathematical relationships and situations.

Examples

- Physical: objects and action on them
- Visual: a ten frame or hundred chart
- Abstract: an open number line

Handout 2.3 shows a concept web for addition and subtraction with the three domains of a learning landscape as the branches. This web will serve as a record of the components you identify.

Record some components related to each domain by adding branches to the diagram.

Share your components with each other. Be sure to ask questions so that everyone has a common understanding of the ideas. It may also be helpful to spend some time developing consistent language to describe the components in the three domains.

You will add to this list of components periodically as you move through the sessions in this *Teaching by Design* volume. It is not necessary to completely fill in the concept web at this point. Just be sure to capture the ideas you have so far based on your professional experience at this grade level. This is a document you will return to often, so be sure to staple or tape it in a well-marked place in your journal.

Activity 2.4 Before the Next Session

5 minutes   Handout 2.4 Student Connections: Observing Counting Strategies

Before the next session, use several of the counting tasks on Handout 2.4 to observe three students engaging in mathematics. Ideally, you will include the two children you described in Activity 2.1 and at least one additional student. The purpose of this and other Student Connections activities is for you to collect some data about your students that will be shared at the next meeting.

Handout 2.4 contains a range of counting tasks. You do not need to ask each student to complete all of the tasks. Instead, start by selecting a task you believe to be within the reach of the student you are observing. If the student is successful, move to one of the following tasks in the sequence. If the student struggles, try adjusting the numbers in the task or move to a task earlier in the sequence. Your objective in conducting these interviews is to find the limit for each student.

Sit with each student as they complete the sequence of tasks you select on Handout 2.4 and record what they say and do. When you collect observational data with each student, try to be as detailed as possible in describing how they approach the task, how difficult the task is for your students, what errors they make, and anything else of interest that occurs during the observation.

Activity 2.5 Lesson Design Notes

5 minutes

The key ideas for this session are

- A learning landscape can function as a map of student learning for teachers.
- A learning landscape includes three domains: (1) strategies, (2) big ideas, and (3) mathematical models.

Reflect on the connections you see between the learning landscape and the three themes that organize the Lesson Design Notes.

- How might the learning landscape help you to answer the question: *Where do you want to go?*
- What might the models or strategies that students use tell you about their current understanding? How might this help you answer the question: *Where are you now?*

References and Resources

Dolk, M., & Fosnot, C. T. (2006). *Fostering children's mathematical development: The landscape of learning* [CD-ROM]. Portsmouth, NH: Heinemann.

Fosnot, C. T., & Dolk, M. (2001). *Young mathematicians at work: Constructing number sense, addition, and subtraction.* Portsmouth, NH: Heinemann.

Van de Walle, J. A. (2009). *Elementary and middle school mathematics: Teaching developmentally* (7th ed.). Needham Heights, MA: Allyn & Bacon.

Handout 2.1

Getting From Here to There

	Maps	Turn-by-Turn Directions
How are they the same?		
Advantages/benefits		
Disadvantages/negatives		

Dot Cards

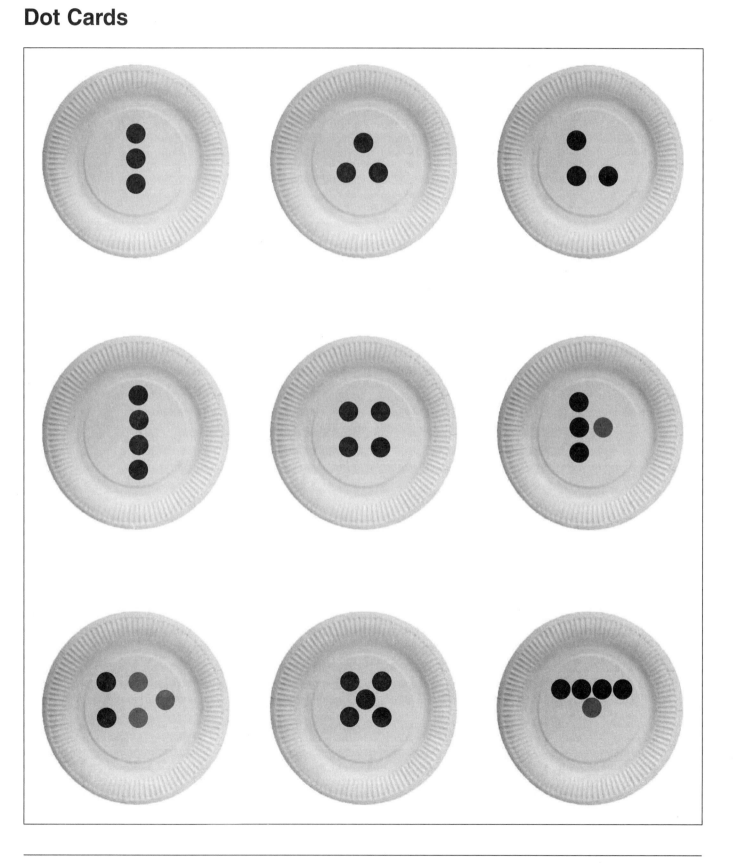

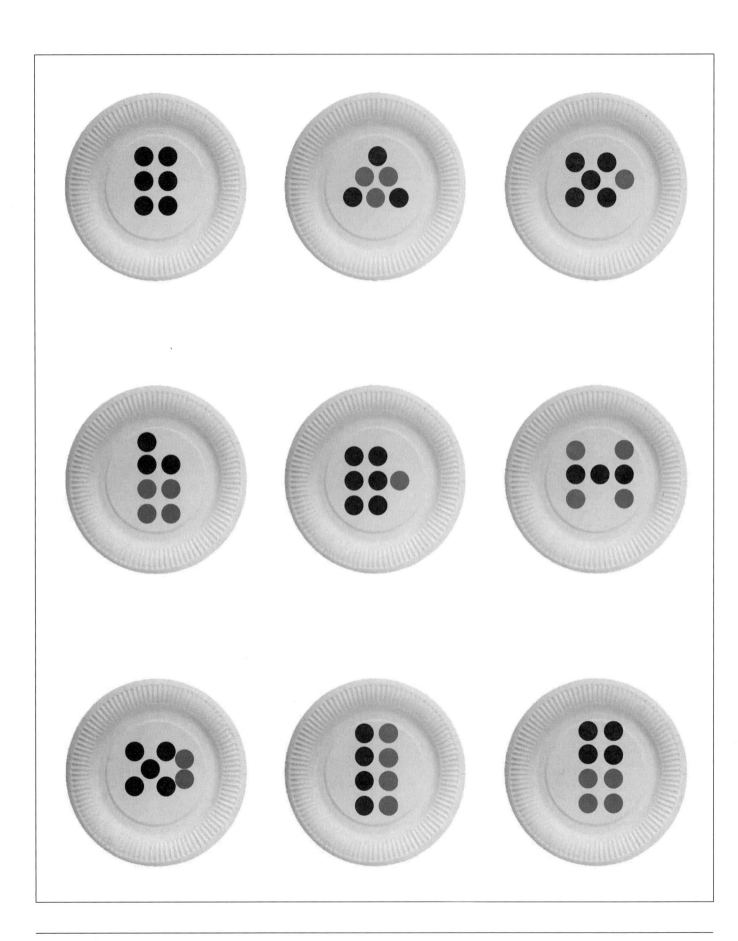

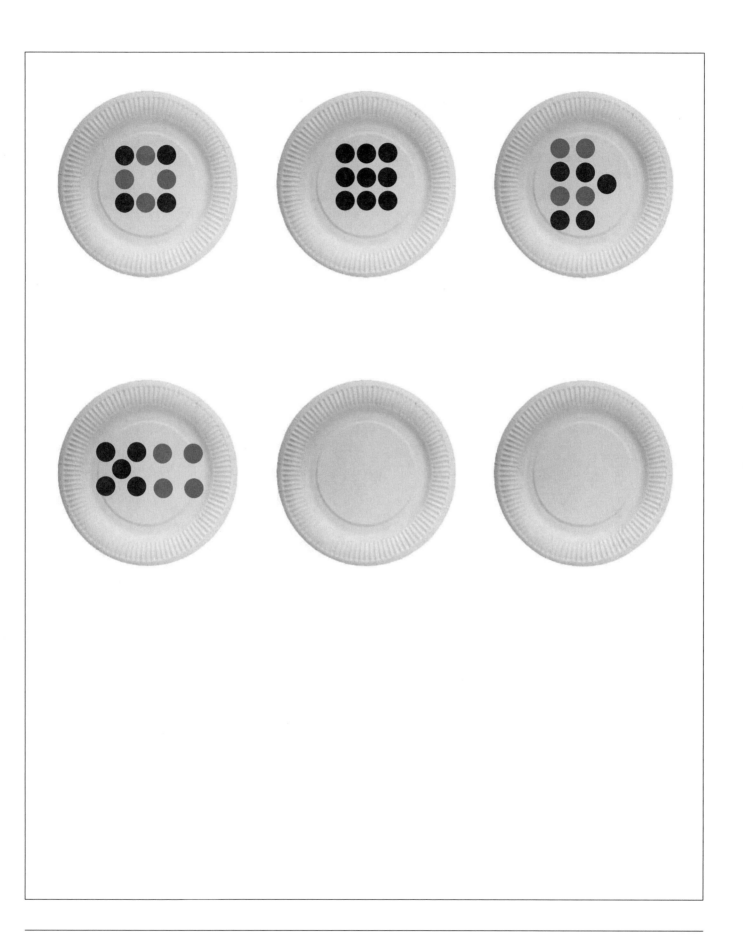

Handout 2.3
Components of a Learning Landscape: Addition and Subtraction

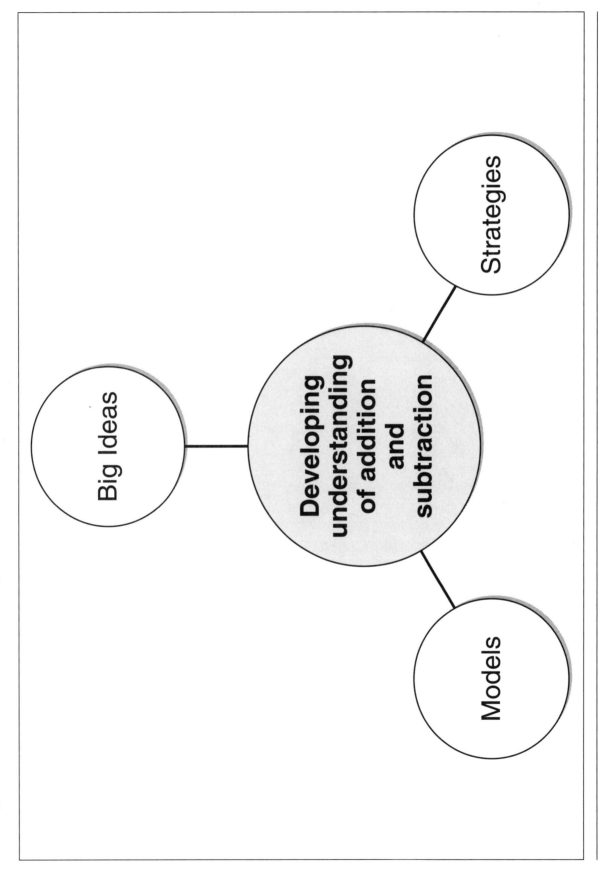

Handout 2.4
Student Connections

Observing Counting Strategies

For all of the following tasks, you will need a writing instrument. You will also need to prepare the following materials for tasks G through K:

- 50 counters—any type (cubes, blocks, tokens, paper clips)
- 3 containers—any type (bags, boxes, tubs) filled with counters as follows:
  - Place 8 counters in the first container
  - Place 17 counters in the second container
  - Place 25 counters in the third container

This handout contains a range of counting tasks. You do not need to ask each student to complete all the tasks. Instead, start by selecting a task you believe to be within the reach of the student you are observing. If the student is successful, move to one of the following tasks in the sequence. If the student struggles, try adapting the numbers in the task or move to a task earlier in the sequence. Your objective in conducting these interviews is to find the limit for each student.

Note that there are *two* sequences here: the first (A–F) focuses on oral counting and the second (G–K) focuses on one-to-one correspondence in counting objects.

No counters required for tasks A through F

Verbal Counting	
Task A	*Can you count to 10?*
Student 1	
Student 2	
Student 3	
Task B	*Can you count to 20?*
Student 1	
Student 2	
Student 3	

Task C	Can you count backward starting at 10?
Student 1	
Student 2	
Student 3	
Task D	Can you to 100 by 10s?
Student 1	
Student 2	
Student 3	
Task E	Can you count from 14 to 27?
Student 1	
Student 2	
Student 3	
Task F	Can you count on from 137 by 10s?
Student 1	
Student 2	
Student 3	

Prepared counters required for tasks G through K

Counting Objects	
Task G	Give the student the container with 8 counters.
	How many counters are in this bag? You may take them out.
Student 1	
Student 2	
Student 3	
Task H	Give the student the container with 17 counters.
	How many counters are in this container?
Student 1	
Student 2	
Student 3	
Task I	Give the student the container with 20 counters.
	Please take 7 counters out of this container and put them on the table.
Student 1	
Student 2	
Student 3	

Task J	Put the counters back into the container.
	Please take 14 counters out of this container and put them on the table.
Student 1	
Student 2	
Student 3	
Task K	Leave the counters from the previous task on the table.
	Please put 20 counters on the table.
Student 1	
Student 2	
Student 3	

Session 3

Counting and Number Concepts

How do children develop skill with counting and number concepts?

Description

Learning to count is a complex and important process that forms the basis of children's ability to develop strategies for addition and subtraction. Children attain fluency with verbal counting, counting objects, and number concepts through a variety of learning experiences.

Key Ideas

- Counting is the basis of children's ability to add and subtract.
- Developing strategies for keeping track of the objects being counted is an important landmark in student learning.
- The structure of a ten frame can help students develop an understanding of number concepts.
- One-on-one student interviews can provide considerable insight into what children know and can do.

Outline of Activities

- 3.1 Counting and Number Sense   (30 minutes)
- 3.2 Discussing Student Connections   (15 minutes)
- 3.3 Conducting Student Interviews   (15 minutes)
- 3.4 Developing Number Concepts   (20 minutes)
- 3.5 Before the Next Session   (5 minutes)
- 3.6 Lesson Design Notes   (5 minutes)

What to Bring

- Journals (and writing instruments)
- Notes and student work: Student Connections activity (Handout 2.4)

To Complete Before Session 4

- Student Connections: Comparing and Ordering Tasks (Handout 3.5)

Facilitator Notes   Session 3

Counting and Number Concepts

If this is your first time facilitating the group, please refer to the more detailed facilitator guidelines in the Introduction. As the facilitator, it is generally your job to keep the conversation flowing and watch the clock. Use your judgment to decide when it's appropriate to extend a session for good conversation or when it's time to move on to the next activity. Remember to keep the group norms posted and revise them, as a group, as necessary.

Before the Session

- Make copies of the following handouts for each team member:
    - ☐ 3.1A Counting Stories
    - ☐ 3.1B Number Concepts: Counting
    - ☐ 3.4 Representing Numbers With a Ten Frame
    - ☐ 3.5 Student Connections: Comparing and Ordering Tasks
- Gather the following materials to be used in this session:
    - ☐ Group norms (from Activity 1.4)
    - ☐ One or two pairs of scissors
    - ☐ Chart paper
    - ☐ Markers
    - ☐ Counters
- Remind team members to bring the following items from previous sessions:
    - ☐ Journal (and writing instruments)
    - ☐ Completed homework, Handout 2.4 Student Connections: Observing Counting Strategies

During the Session

- Post group norms, and revise as a group as necessary.
- Activity 3.1: facilitate partnering, if necessary; lead brainstorming, and serve as recorder of ideas.
- Activity 3.3: lead brainstorming, and serve as recorder of ideas.
- Activity 3.4: facilitate partnering, if necessary.

After the Session

- Remind team members of homework, Handout 3.5 Student Connections: Comparing and Ordering Tasks.
- Pass any team materials on to the next facilitator.

Activity 3.1 Counting and Number Sense

30 minutes

Handout 3.1A Counting Stories
Handout 3.1B Number Concepts: Counting
Chart paper and markers
Scissors

Counting is a skill that is easy to take for granted, but it is the foundation for understanding number and learning addition and subtraction (Kilpatrick, Swafford, & Findell, 2001). When children learn to count, there are two areas of development: (1) fluency with verbal counting and (2) the ability to accurately and reliably count collections of objects (Van de Walle, 2009). Skill with the first area does not guarantee skill with the second. In fact, children's ability to recite the counting sequence from memory can sometimes mask missing pieces in their knowledge of number (Fosnot & Dolk, 2001). Teachers who carefully observe students at work on counting tasks can begin to recognize landmarks in children's counting.

Read the student vignettes on Handout 3.1A Counting Stories.

Discuss the vignettes on Handout 3.1A with a partner. Sort the vignettes in two piles: (1) students with counting fluency and (2) students who have difficulty with counting.

As you work together, consider the following questions:

- Does the student in this vignette have fluency with verbal counting? What is your evidence?

- Does the student in this vignette have the ability to accurately count each collection of objects? What is your evidence?

- For students who do not demonstrate accurate counting skills, what are their specific difficulties?

Share your sorting with the group. How much agreement and disagreement did your group have in your sorting? What observations did each pair make about the students? What questions do you have about these children?

Read the descriptions of number concepts for counting listed on Handout 3.1B. Did you use any of these terms in your discussion of the students? Which terms apply to some of the strategies described in the vignettes? Which terms are included as components of the learning landscape that you developed in Session 2 (Handout 2.3)? Which terms could be added?

Students develop their understanding of counting and number primarily through practice (Baroody, 1998). Teachers and researchers have found that providing a variety of meaningful counting experiences is the key to helping children develop their counting abilities (Clements, 2004; Van de Walle, 2009).

Brainstorm a list of tasks or activities that might help the students who have not yet mastered counting tasks, such as the ones from the vignettes and the students you observed for the Student Connections activity (Handout 2.4). Keep track of your group's ideas on chart paper.

Discuss the following questions after generating the list:

- How do the activities help students develop strategies for keeping track as they are counting?

- How do the activities provide opportunities for meaningful practice?
- What approaches might help students identify counting errors in a nonthreatening way?

Record ideas from the discussion in your Lesson Design Notes. Are there ideas that came up in your discussion of counting tasks that have general implications for the design of mathematics lessons?

Activity 3.2 Discussing Student Connections

15 minutes   Handout 2.4 Student Connections: Observing Counting Strategies

Read your completed Student Connections Handout 2.4 from Session 2. How do the terms on Handout 3.1B help you to better understand your students' skills and difficulties with counting? Which of your students demonstrated similar strategies or misconceptions as the students in the vignettes on Handout 3.1A?

Share with the group the strategies or errors that your students made. Which are similar to the ones discussed in the previous vignettes? Which are different? Ask the group to provide input on the students with different strategies and errors.

- Does the student you describe have fluency with the forward number sequence? What is your evidence?
- Does the student you describe have the ability to accurately count this collection of objects? What is your evidence?
- For students who have not demonstrated these skills, what are their specific difficulties?

Activity 3.3 Conducting Student Interviews

15 minutes

A powerful way to gather formative assessment data about students is through individual interviews. A one-on-one interview provides considerable insight into what children know and can do. Interviews allow the teacher to engage in conversation with each child to determine the extent of knowledge and the relative sophistication of the child's numerical strategies. By asking probing questions, teachers can encourage students to clarify their interpretations of the problem and their responses. During the interview, a teacher gathers data about the problem-solving strategies and thinking processes that students use to approach each problem. By interviewing many students, teachers gather information about the misconceptions their student have and the range of strategies that they use to solve mathematics problems.

Interviews provide teachers with a detailed picture of children's mathematical understanding and therefore help them to improve their practice (Buschman, 2001). However, conducting one-on-one interviews also presents some challenges. It takes specialized skill and practice to become proficient in using interviews to guide instruction.

Reflect on the three student interviews you conducted. What new insights do you have about these children? What new questions do you have about their skill in and understanding of counting? What went well with the interview? What challenges did you face?

Brainstorm a list of suggestions for conducting student interviews based on your shared responses to the previous questions. What advice do you have for yourself or for a colleague who might embark on mathematical interviews with students?

Read the following suggestions for conducting student interviews that come from mathematics education experts.

Prepare for the interviews.

Choose a private location where distractions can be minimized. Try to ensure that you and the children will not be interrupted during the interviews. Provide a range of tools, including various manipulatives, pencils, paper, and so on.

Select tasks and problems with care.

Pose a problem that will challenge students. Prepare several tasks that range in difficulty. If the student quickly solves the problem, provide a more challenging problem. If the student cannot complete the given tasks, try one that is slightly easier. However, be sure to provide enough time for students to struggle and make sense of the problem. You may also suggest that they try using a different tool before moving to an easier task.

Listen carefully.

The child should do most of the talking, not you. Of course, you have to ask penetrating questions, but you should spend most of your time listening to what the child has to say and observing. If you are talking more than the child, something is wrong. Try to search for the child's point of view. Extending or expanding a child's thinking is difficult until you first determine how a child approaches the problem. Most children also think differently than adults do, which means that seeing the problem from a child's point of view can be challenging.

Ask the right questions.

Phrase your questions in a neutral way so as to avoid suggesting an answer to a child. Pay attention to non-verbal cues as well—tone and facial expressions can be quite revealing. Start with open-ended questions, then proceed to more specific questions as you gain insight into the reasons behind children's thinking. Some questions you may consider include, "How did you think about this problem?" or, "What did you do to get this answer?"

Don't correct and teach.

When a student makes a mistake or has an incorrect solution, your goal is to determine the child's mathematical thinking, not to correct thinking. Later on, you will have an opportunity to use what you learned in the interview to help the child. Refrain from correcting and teaching. Avoid saying, "No, you're wrong; this is how to do it." Don't show disapproval by grimacing or scowling. Instead, convey your interest in what the child said, even if it is wrong, and that you want to find out more about it.

Sources: Ginsburg, Jacobs, & Lopez, 1998; Buschman, 2001.

Discuss the following questions:

- How does your list compare to this list?

- Which suggestions do you think are the most helpful for you?

- When you consider both your list and the items from the mathematics education experts, what are some of the challenges you might face in attempting to abide by these guidelines?

Activity 3.4 Developing Number Concepts

20 minutes

Handout 2.3 Components of a Learning Landscape
Handout 3.4 Representing Numbers With a Ten Frame
Counters

When students use objects to solve problems, they initially do so in an unstructured way. One way to help students build strong number sense is to introduce models with structures that can help them develop an understanding of number relationships and emphasize important numerical understanding such as organizing with 10s. One model that you may have included in your components of a learning landscape from Session 2 is a ten frame.

A ten frame is a two by five array that provides spaces in which students can place manipulatives. By arranging the objects in the array, they can see relationships that would not otherwise be obvious. In particular, the ten frame may help students to see numbers in relation to five and ten, which is a helpful strategy for gaining fluency with addition and subtraction (Fosnot & Dolk, 2001).

Work with a partner to create quantities using the colored counters on the ten frames on the front of Handout 3.4. Each person discretely fills in the ten frame with a quantity and keeps it covered so that the partner cannot see the frame. Take turns doing a "quick peek," showing the ten frame to your partner for a few seconds before covering it up again. Do this several times.

Discuss the following questions with your group:

- What strategies did you use to figure out how many counters were on the ten frames?

- Van de Walle (2009) suggests that teachers should provide students with practice using the ten frame rather than practicing procedures. It is through continued use of the ten frame that students learn the relationships between numbers and the ability to visualize numbers quickly. What is your reaction to this suggestion? Do you think that practice using a ten frame would help students develop fluency with number combinations? In what ways?

- Have you used ten frames with your students? If so, what have you observed about how student learning is influenced by using this model?

- How might the students in the vignettes on Handout 3.1A have responded differently to the counting objects tasks if they had been encouraged to use ten frames for the tasks?

- What additional strategies and big ideas on the learning landscape (Handout 2.3) might students develop through the use of a ten frame model?

Activity 3.5 Before the Next Session

5 minutes   Handout 3.5 Student Connections: Comparing and Ordering Tasks

Before the next session, interview three children using some of the comparing and ordering tasks shown on Handout 3.5. You may interview the same three children you interviewed after Session 2 or you may choose to interview different children this time. Choose students of varied ability levels. Remember that the purpose of this and other Student Connections in this volume is for you to collect some data about your students that will be shared at the next meeting.

As in the last student data collection, you do not need to ask each student to complete all the tasks. Instead, start by selecting a task you believe to be within the reach of the student you are observing. If the student is successful, move to one of the following tasks in the sequence. If the student struggles, try adapting the numbers in the task or move to a task earlier in the sequence. Your objective in conducting these interviews is to find the limit for each student. Sit with students individually as they complete the selected tasks on Handout 3.5 and record what they say and do. Try to be as detailed as possible in describing how they approach each task, how difficult the task is for your students, what errors they make, and any other points of interest during the interview.

Activity 3.6 Lesson Design Notes

5 minutes

The key ideas for this session are

- Counting is the basis of children's ability to add and subtract.
- Developing strategies for keeping track of the objects being counted is an important landmark in student learning.
- The structure of a ten frame can help students develop an understanding of number concepts.
- One-on-one student interviews can provide considerable insight into what children know and can do.

Reflect on what you learned during this session and how the ideas apply to each of the three themes in your Lesson Design Notes (Handout 1.3). A few prompts related to two of the themes follow. These are merely suggestions and should not limit your reflection or the ideas you capture.

- Where do you want to go?
- Where are you now?
  - o In Activity 3.2, you discussed student connections. What new insights do you have about student understanding of counting concepts?
- What is the best way to get there?
  - o In Activity 3.4, you examined ten frames. What mathematical concepts can ten frames help students understand?
  - o In Activity 3.1, you explored counting concepts. Add the tasks that you and your team brainstormed that would help students develop counting concepts.

References and Resources

Baroody. A. J. (with Coslick, R. T.). (1998). *Fostering children's mathematical power: An investigative approach to K–8 mathematics instruction.* Mahwah, NJ: Lawrence Erlbaum.

Buschman, L. (2001). Using student interviews to guide classroom instruction: An action research project. *Teaching Children Mathematics, 8*(4), 222–227.

Clements, D. H. (2004). Major themes and recommendations. In D. H. Clements, J. Sarama, & A.-M. DiBiase (Eds.), *Engaging young children in mathematics: Standards for early childhood mathematics education,* (pp. 7–72). Mahwah, NJ: Lawrence Erlbaum.

Fosnot, C. T., & Dolk, M. (2001). *Young mathematicians at work: Constructing number sense, addition, and subtraction.* Portsmouth, NH: Heinemann.

Ginsburg, H. P., Jacobs, S., & Lopez, L. (1998). *The teacher's guide to flexible interviewing in the classroom: Learning what children know about math.* Needham Heights, MA: Allyn & Bacon.

Kilpatrick, J., Swafford, J., & Findell, B. (Eds.) (2001). *Adding it up: Helping children learn mathematics.* Washington, DC: National Academies Press.

Van de Walle, J. A. (2009). *Elementary and middle school mathematics: Teaching developmentally* (7th ed.). Needham Heights, MA: Allyn & Bacon.

Handout 3.1A
Counting Stories

Scenario: Ms. Erikson has noticed that some of her students are making errors when they are counting objects. She decided to observe her students as they count a set of objects. She puts a pile of 11 blocks on the table and asks each child: "How many blocks do you have?" For some students, she then puts a pile of 32 blocks on the table and asks the same question.

In this counting task, place these vignettes in order from least skilled to most skilled. You may find it useful to cut the strips apart so that you can move them around while making your determinations.

- -

Marcus looks at the blocks and then looks up. He says, "1, 2, 3, 4, 5, 6, 7, 8, 9, 10, 11, 12, 13, 14, 15" and stops. He does not look at the blocks while he recites the numbers.

Ms. Erikson asks, "Why did you stop at 15?" Marcus looks away and doesn't answer.

- -

Tara begins counting the group of blocks. She touches each one as she says the numbers in the counting sequence, but she does not keep track of which blocks have already been counted. With a puzzled look on her face, she hesitates and stops counting when she gets to 8 . . . "9?"

- -

Lucas starts with the pile of blocks and moves one block to a new pile on the right. He counts "1" and moves one block, "2" and moves another block, and continues until there are no blocks left in the first pile . . . "11."

- -

Dina points at the blocks as she counts, "1, 2, 5, 6, 7, 8, 2, 3, 4, 5, 6—there's 6."

- -

Freddy puts the blocks in a circle and then begins counting. He touches each block and counts it but continues around the circle a second time. He says, "1, 2, 3, 4, 5, 6, 7, 8, 9, 10, 11, 12, 13, 14 . . . 14."

- -

Yanique puts the blocks in a row and then begins counting. She touches two blocks at a time and counts "2, 4, 6, 8, 10." She looks at the remaining block, then looks up and says "11."

- -

Tiffanie, having successfully counted the first pile of blocks, is given the second. She counts "1" and moves one block, "2" and moves another block, and continues until she has reached 10 blocks. At this point, she makes a row of the 10 blocks. She then makes two more rows with 10 blocks each. She counts "10, 20, 30" and, touching each of the remaining blocks not in a row, "31, 32 . . . 32 blocks."

- -

Dakota, having successfully counted the first pile of blocks, is given the second. He puts the blocks in a row and then begins counting. He touches each block and counts it, finishing, "28, 29 . . . twenty-ten, twenty-eleven, twenty-twelve?" He looks confused and uncertain.

- -

Handout 3.1B
Number Concepts: Counting

Cardinality	The number that ends the counting sequence represents how many objects are in the collection.
	A child who understands cardinality knows that the last count answers the question, "How many?"
One-to-one correspondence	A number word is matched with each item in the collection.
	If two collections can be matched item for item, they are equivalent.
	It is necessary to keep track of the objects that have been counted.
Subitize	The number of items in a small collection is quickly recognized and named.
Hierarchical inclusion	Numbers grow by exactly one with each count.
	The numbers in the counting sequence are nested inside each other.
	When one object is removed from a group of six objects, five objects remain.
Counting sequence	The counting words must be recited in a consistent order.
Skip counting	Counting by a number other than one.
	A more efficient counting strategy based on groups, including groups of 10.

Handout 3.4
Representing Numbers With a Ten Frame

Handout 3.5
Student Connections: Comparing and Ordering Tasks

You will need the following materials for the tasks on this page:

- Thirty pennies, tokens, or paperclips.

- Three cups labeled A, B, C, and filled with the objects as follows:
  - Cup A has 12 objects.
  - Cup B has 8 objects.
  - Cup C has 10 objects.

You do not need to ask students to complete all the tasks. Start by selecting tasks you believe to be within the reach of the student you are observing. If the student struggles, try adapting the numbers in the task or move to an earlier task. Your objective is to find the limit for each student.

Note that there are *two* sequences here: the first (A–B) focuses on comparing and ordering groups of objects and the second (C–F) focuses on comparing and ordering written numbers.

Task A	Give the student cup A and cup B
	Which cup has more objects? How do you know that it has more?
Student 1	
Student 2	
Student 3	
Task B	Give the student all three cups.
	Put the cups in order so the first cup has the least amount and the last cup has the most objects.
Student 1	
Student 2	
Student 3	

You will need the following materials for the tasks on this page:

- Three index cards or sticky notes.
- Write one of these numbers on each card: 4, 7, and 11.

Task C	Give the student the cards 4 and 7.
	Which card shows the larger number? How do you know?
Student 1	
Student 2	
Student 3	
Task D	Give the student all three cards.
	Put these three cards in number order. Place the card showing the smallest number here and the card showing the largest number here.
Student 1	
Student 2	
Student 3	

You will need the following materials for the tasks on this page:

- Four index cards or sticky notes.
- Write one of these numbers on each card: 24, 34, 37, and 42.

Task E	Give the student the cards 24, 34, and 42.
	Which card shows the largest number? How do you know?
Student 1	
Student 2	
Student 3	
Task F	Give the student all four cards.
	Put these four cards in number order. Place the card showing the smallest number here and the card showing the largest number here.
Student 1	
Student 2	
Student 3	

Session **4**

Comparing and Ordering Numbers

How do students learn how to compare and order numbers?

Description

Children gradually develop the ability to compare numbers and put them in order based on their experiences comparing and ordering with sets of objects, along with their knowledge of place value as they develop the ability to work with larger numbers. Children need opportunities to practice their skills in comparing and ordering numbers in many different contexts.

Key Ideas

- Researchers have identified a learning progression describing the typical development for K–1 students.

- Mathematics games provide opportunities to practice comparing and ordering skills.

- The Standards for Mathematical Practice in the Common Core State Standards identify areas of instructional emphasis and help to make connections between different mathematical concepts and processes.

- When instruction focuses on a small number of key areas of emphasis, students gain extended experience with core concepts and skills.

Outline of Activities

- 4.1 Learning Progression for Comparing and Ordering   (15 minutes)
- 4.2 Discussing Student Connections   (15 minutes)
- 4.3 Mathematics Games   (30 minutes)
- 4.4 The Common Core State Standards   (20 minutes)
- 4.5 Before the Next Session   (5 minutes)
- 4.6 Lesson Design Notes   (5 minutes)

What to Bring

- Journal (and writing instruments)
- Notes and student work: Student Connections activity (Handout 3.5)

To Complete Before Session 5

- Investigating Instructional Materials activity for addition or subtraction
- Student Connections: Observing Students Playing Games (Handout 4.5)

Facilitator Notes   Session 4

Comparing and Ordering Numbers

If this is your first time facilitating the group, please refer to the more detailed facilitator guidelines in the Introduction. As the facilitator, it is generally your job to keep the conversation flowing and watch the clock. Use your judgment to decide when it's appropriate to extend a session for good conversation or when it's time to move on to the next activity. Remember to keep the group norms posted and revise them, as a group, as necessary.

Before the Session

- Make copies of the following handouts for each team member:
    - ☐ 4.3 Compare and Order Games
    - ☐ 4.4 Common Core State Standards
    - ☐ 4.5 Student Connections: Observing Students Playing Games
- Gather the following materials to be used in this session:
    - ☐ Group norms (from Activity 1.4)
    - ☐ Manipulatives (blocks or other counters)
    - ☐ Dot cards (or plates from previous session)
    - ☐ Number cards
    - ☐ Chart paper
    - ☐ Markers
- Remind team members to bring the following items from previous sessions:
    - ☐ Journal (and writing instruments)
    - ☐ Completed homework, Handout 3.5 Student Connections: Comparing and Ordering Tasks

During the Session

- Post group norms, and revise as a group as necessary.
- Activity 4.3: lead brainstorming, and serve as recorder of ideas; facilitate partnering, if necessary.

After the Session

- Remind team members of homework, Identifying Instructional Materials activity for addition or subtraction and Handout 4.5 Student Connections: Observing Students Playing Games.
- Pass any team materials on to the next facilitator.

Activity 4.1 Learning Progression for Comparing and Ordering

15 minutes

Children develop the ability to compare and order numbers based on their prior experiences learning the number sequence for verbal counting, counting objects, and, later, their place value knowledge. The ability to compare and order numbers is an important milestone in students' understanding of the number system.

Discuss the challenges of learning how to compare and order numbers.

- What stumbling blocks have you observed students encounter when learning to compare and order numbers?
- What is surprising or puzzling to you about the challenges students face when learning to compare and order numbers?
- What questions do you have about the ways that students approach comparing and ordering tasks?

Read the following descriptions of the stages of the learning progression for comparing and ordering numbers. Illustrate each one by acting out, drawing, or providing a specific example of what is being described.

Even students who can count fluently may not understand that the numbers in the sequence are in order according to their magnitude and that the number that comes after another number is one larger. These concepts are important landmarks for kindergarten (Baroody, 2004).

When comparing quantities, most children start out by making *visual comparisons* of groups of objects. They are likely to base their comparisons on attributes that are not related to quantity, such as the colors of the objects or which group takes up more space (Carpenter, Fennema, Franke, Levi, & Empson, 1999). Students at this stage can only compare quantities that are visibly different from each other (Griffin, 2005).

When children develop an understanding of one-to-one correspondence, they are able to use *matching* to make comparisons (Van de Walle, 2009). For example, you may have noticed students who line up the objects from two groups in order to compare them. Students who use matching to compare can only compare quantities that are physically adjacent to each other (Griffin, 2005).

Some students may not use matching, but move directly from visual comparisons to *counting* (Van de Walle, 2009). Children will now count the objects in each group to determine which one has more or less (Clements, 2004). In addition, students are now able to link numbers to quantities, and can tell which of two numerals is bigger or smaller (Griffin, 2005).

When children develop understanding of the underlying structure of the decimal numeration system, they are able to incorporate *place value* in making comparisons. The idea that position is critical to the value of a digit is fairly abstract, but it is developmentally appropriate with proper instruction as early as kindergarten (Baroody, 1998).

As you were discussing each stage of the learning progression with your group, you may have made some connections with the students that you recently interviewed. In the next activity, you will use this learning progression to describe your students' understanding of comparing and ordering numbers.

Keep this continuum of strategies in mind as you discuss your student connections in the next activity.

Activity 4.2 Discussing Student Connections

15 minutes   Handout 3.5 Student Connections: Comparing and Ordering Tasks

Read your completed Student Connections Handout 3.5 from Session 3. Did your students use any of the strategies described in the learning progression in the previous activity?

Share with your group the strategies your students used. Are there any approaches that are different from ones that have been discussed in today's session? Was there anything that surprised you?

Discuss the following questions:

- What new insights do you have about your students?

- What additional questions or tasks would you pose next to get more information about what these students understand about comparing and ordering?

- What instructional strategies might help the struggling students you interviewed?

Activity 4.3 Mathematics Games

30 minutes   Handout 4.3 Compare and Order Games

Number games can provide opportunities for students to build their understanding of number and operations. They can be a motivating and engaging way for students to practice skills. Games also help students become more independent—the players decide when an answer is correct, rather than relying on the teacher to validate it.

Brainstorm a list of math games your students like to play. Use chart paper or a white board to keep track of the games mentioned and write the names of the people who suggest them. If you are not familiar with a game that is mentioned, ask that group member to describe it to you.

Discuss the benefits you have observed when students play math games. Do you agree with the following quotation?

> There are many different things the teacher can do, but playing with individual children or a small group is the most useful activity for the teacher. The reason is that playing games with children is the best way to assess their level of numerical reasoning.
>
> Constance Kamii,
> *Young Children Reinvent Arithmetic* (2000, p. 213)

Read the descriptions of the three games on Handout 4.3 Compare and Order Games. Each of these games engages students in a context for comparing and ordering quantities or numbers.

Play each of the games with a partner. The third game is a three-person game, so play it as if you have an imaginary third person.

Discuss each game with your partner using the following questions:

- How does this game support understanding of comparing and ordering numbers?
- What variations could you make that would make the game more or less challenging for some of your students?
- What questions would you ask students as they play, or after the game is finished, to find out about their mathematical learning?
- What would you look for as you observe students?

Share your partner discussion with the group.

Activity 4.4 The Common Core State Standards

20 minutes   Handout 4.4 Common Core State Standards

Discuss the following questions with your group:

- Have you heard or used the phrase, *a mile wide and an inch deep* when talking about curriculum? What does this phrase mean to you?
- How well does this phrase describe your own experience as a mathematical learner?
- What are the problems associated with curriculum that cover lots of topics, but none in depth?

Read the following excerpt from the Introduction to the Common Core State Standards for Mathematics.

> For over a decade, research studies of mathematics education in high-performing countries have pointed to the conclusion that the mathematics curriculum in the United States must become substantially more focused and coherent in order to improve mathematics achievement in this country. To deliver on the promise of common standards, the standards must address the problem of a curriculum that is "a mile wide and an inch deep." These Standards are a substantial answer to that challenge.
>
> It is important to recognize that "fewer standards" are no substitute for focused standards. Achieving "fewer standards" would be easy to do by resorting to broad, general statements. Instead, these Standards aim for clarity and specificity.
>
> Assessing the coherence of a set of standards is more difficult than assessing their focus. William Schmidt and Richard Houang (2002) have said that content standards and curricula are coherent if they are:
>
> > articulated over time as a sequence of topics and performances that are logical and reflect, where appropriate, the sequential or hierarchical nature of the disciplinary content from which the subject matter derives. That is, what and how students are taught should reflect not only the topics that fall within a certain academic discipline,

but also the key ideas [emphasis added] that determine how knowledge is organized and generated within that discipline. This implies that "to be coherent," a set of content standards must evolve from particulars (e.g., the meaning and operations of whole numbers, including simple math facts and routine computational procedures associated with whole numbers and fractions) to deeper structures inherent in the discipline. These deeper structures then serve as a means for connecting the particulars (such as an understanding of the rational number system and its properties).

These Standards endeavor to follow such a design, not only by stressing conceptual understanding of key ideas, but also by continually returning to organizing principles such as place value or the laws of arithmetic to structure those ideas.

In addition, the "sequence of topics and performances" that is outlined in a body of mathematics standards must also respect what is known about how students learn. As Confrey (2007) points out, developing "sequenced obstacles and challenges for students . . . absent the insights about meaning that derive from careful study of learning, would be unfortunate and unwise." In recognition of this, the development of these Standards began with research-based learning progressions detailing what is known today about how students' mathematical knowledge, skill, and understanding develop over time.

Source: National Governors Association Center for Best Practices and Council of Chief State School Officers (2010, p. 3).

Discuss the following questions with your group:

- How do the Common Core State Standards attempt to address the problem of a curriculum that is "a mile wide and an inch deep"?
- What does it mean to have content standards that are coherent?

The Common Core State Standards for Mathematics begin with eight "Standards for Mathematical Practice." These standards describe processes and proficiencies with longstanding importance in mathematics and apply across all of the grades from kindergarten to Grade 12.

Read the Standards for Mathematical Practice (Handout 4.4).

Write in your journal, in response to the following questions:

- Which of the eight standards have you intentionally designed instruction to support?
- Which of the eight standards are challenging to teach and not typically present in your classroom?
- What ideas do you have increasing students' opportunities to develop and use the practices described by these standards?

Share with your group your responses to the third question in the preceding list.

If you do not have a copy of the Common Core State Standards for Mathematics for your grade, go to the website at http://www.corestandards.org/ and print a copy. The document includes "Standards for Mathematical Content" for each grade level from kindergarten through high school. You will use it as a resource in subsequent sessions. If you would like to learn more about the Common Core State Standards, review other documentation provided on the website. For example, the "Myths and Facts" document and the FAQ section provide helpful information.

Activity 4.5 Before the Next Session

5 minutes

Handout 4.3 Compare and Order Games
Handout 4.5 Student Connections: Observing Students Playing Games
Materials for game (see Handout 4.3)

Instructional Materials for Addition or Subtraction

In Session 5, you will be analyzing lessons that address counting (kindergarten) or subtraction (first grade). Between now and the next session, identify a counting or subtraction lesson from your instructional materials. You might select a lesson that you have not taught before, one that you particularly enjoy teaching, or one that is challenging to teach.

The activity in Session 5 will focus on these questions:

- What big ideas, strategies, and mathematical models are being developed in the lesson?
- What skills and knowledge are required to complete the tasks?
- What are the important mathematical concepts underlying the lesson?
- What are the strengths of the lesson?
- What are some limitations, questions, and concerns that you have about the lesson?

Observing Students Playing Games

Before the next session, select one of the games from Handout 4.3 to play with three small groups of students. Sit with each group as they play the game and record what they say and do. Record your observations on Handout 4.5, and try to be as detailed as possible in describing how they approach the game, how difficult it is for them, what errors they make, and anything else of interest that happens during the observation.

Write in your journal about what you learned about student thinking while observing them playing this game. What approaches did the children use? Was there anything that surprised you? How will you use this information to design learning experiences for your students on comparing and ordering quantities and numbers?

Keep your notes and written reflection for the lesson planning process, which will begin in Session 11.

Activity 4.6 Lesson Design Notes

5 minutes

The key ideas for this session are

- Understanding the order of the number sequence is an important landmark for kindergarten students.
- Mathematics games provide opportunities for students to practice comparing and ordering skills.

- The Standards for Mathematical Practice in the Common Core Standards identify areas of instructional emphasis and help to make connections between different mathematical concepts and processes.
- When instruction focuses on a small number of key areas of emphasis, students gain extended experience with core concepts and skills.

Reflect on what you learned during this session and how the ideas apply to each of the three themes in your Lesson Design Notes. A few prompts related to the themes follow. These are merely suggestions and should not limit your reflection or the ideas you capture.

- Where do you want to go?
  - In Activity 4.4, you discussed the Common Core State Standards. What connections do you see between the standards and your notes related to this question? What ideas from the standards can be included in your notes?

- Where are you now?
  - In Activity 4.1, you examined the ways in which students develop understanding of comparing and ordering. Are there any insights from this process that will inform how you identify your students' current knowledge about a mathematical concept?

- What is the best way to get there?
  - In Activity 4.3, you tried out and discussed mathematics games. How can games support students in building understanding for comparing and ordering numbers?

References and Resources

Baroody. A. J. (with Coslick, R. T.). (1998). *Fostering children's mathematical power: An investigative approach to K-8 mathematics instruction.* Mahwah, NJ: Lawrence Erlbaum.

Baroody, A. J. (2004). The developmental bases for early childhood number and operations standards. In D. H. Clements, J. Sarama, & A.-M. DiBiase (Eds.), *Engaging young children in mathematics: Standards for early childhood mathematics education* (pp. 173–219). Mahwah, NJ: Lawrence Erlbaum.

Carpenter, T. P., Fennema, E., Franke, M. L., Levi, L., & Empson, S. B. (1999). *Children's mathematics: Cognitively guided instruction.* Portsmouth, NH: Heinemann.

Clements, D. H. (2004). Major themes and recommendations. In D. H. Clements, J. Sarama, & A.-M. DiBiase (Eds.), *Engaging young children in mathematics: Standards for early childhood mathematics education* (pp. 7–72). Mahwah, NJ: Lawrence Erlbaum.

Griffin, S. (2005). Fostering the development of whole number sense: Teaching mathematics in the primary grades. In M. S. Donovan & J. D. Bransford (Eds.), *How students learn: Mathematics in the classroom* (pp. 257–308). Washington, DC: National Academies Press.

Kamii, C. (with Houseman, L. B.). (2000). *Young children reinvent arithmetic: Implications of Piaget's theory* (2nd ed.). New York: Teachers College Press.

National Governors Association Center for Best Practices, & Council of Chief State School Officers. (2010). *Common Core State Standards: Mathematics.* Retrieved from http://www.corestandards.org/the-standards/mathematics/

Van de Walle, J. A. (2009). *Elementary and middle school mathematics: Teaching developmentally* (7th ed.). Needham Heights, MA: Allyn & Bacon.

Handout 4.3
Compare and Order Games (Three Games)

Grab, Count, and Compare

Materials: Container, small counters, paper plates, paper and pencil

Groups: To be played in groups of two or three students

- Students each grab a handful of items from a container and place them on their individual paper plate.

- Students count their own objects, then trade plates and count the partner's objects.

- Students compare results and discuss which is more.

- For students who are ready to record their work: each student draws a picture to show how many objects each partner has and makes an *x* on the collection that has the most.

- For students who are writing numbers: each student writes the numerals below the pictures.

Sample drawing:

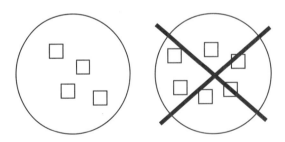

Which is Larger?

Materials: A deck of about 20 dot cards (the deck includes only numbers the students know, and may have multiple cards with the same number). Make a personalized deck using index cards and adhesive dots.

Groups: To be played in groups of two students

- Two students evenly divide the deck of dot cards and mix them up.
- Students each place all of their own cards face down in front of them in a line or an array.
- Students each turn over one of their own cards.
- The students decide who has the card with the larger number.
- The student with the larger number keeps both cards.
- If the cards are the same, the cards stay face up on the table and will be claimed by the person with the highest value card in the next round.

Sample: **Player 1** **Player 2**

For students familiar with numbers, change to number cards (a hybrid could be used as an intermediate step - cards with dots and numbers).

Sample: **Player 1** **Player 2**

As students gain more experience, use more cards and larger numbers.

In Between

Materials: A deck of about 30 dot cards (the deck includes only numbers the students know, and may have multiple cards with the same number). Make a personalized deck using index cards and adhesive dots.

Groups: To be played in groups of three students

- Three students evenly divide the deck of dot cards and mix them up.
- Students each place all of their own cards in a pile face down in front of them.
- Students each turn over their top card.
- The students place the cards in number order.
- The student who had the card "between" the other two claims all the cards.
- If two or three of the face-up cards match, there is no winner. Players each bury that card in their own deck and turn over the next card.

For students familiar with numbers, change to number cards, or a hybrid could be used as an intermediate step (i.e., cards with dots and numbers). As students gain more experience, use more cards and larger numbers.

Handout 4.4
Common Core State Standards

Mathematics | Standards for Mathematical Practice

The Standards for Mathematical Practice describe varieties of expertise that mathematics educators at all levels should seek to develop in their students. These practices rest on important "processes and proficiencies" with longstanding importance in mathematics education. The first of these are the NCTM process standards of problem solving, reasoning and proof, communication, representation, and connections. The second are the strands of mathematical proficiency specified in the National Research Council's report *Adding It Up:* adaptive reasoning, strategic competence, conceptual understanding (comprehension of mathematical concepts, operations and relations), procedural fluency (skill in carrying out procedures flexibly, accurately, efficiently and appropriately), and productive disposition (habitual inclination to see mathematics as sensible, useful, and worthwhile, coupled with a belief in diligence and one's own efficacy).

1. Make sense of problems and persevere in solving them.

Mathematically proficient students start by explaining to themselves the meaning of a problem and looking for entry points to its solution. They analyze givens, constraints, relationships, and goals. They make conjectures about the form and meaning of the solution and plan a solution pathway rather than simply jumping into a solution attempt. They consider analogous problems, and try special cases and simpler forms of the original problem in order to gain insight into its solution. They monitor and evaluate their progress and change course if necessary. Older students might, depending on the context of the problem, transform algebraic expressions or change the viewing window on their graphing calculator to get the information they need. Mathematically proficient students can explain correspondences between equations, verbal descriptions, tables, and graphs or draw diagrams of important features and relationships, graph data, and search for regularity or trends. Younger students might rely on using concrete objects or pictures to help conceptualize and solve a problem. Mathematically proficient students check their answers to problems using a different method, and they continually ask themselves, "Does this make sense?" They can understand the approaches of others to solving complex problems and identify correspondences between different approaches.

2. Reason abstractly and quantitatively.

Mathematically proficient students make sense of quantities and their relationships in problem situations. They bring two complementary abilities to bear on problems involving quantitative relationships: the ability to *decontextualize*—to abstract a given situation and represent it symbolically and manipulate the representing symbols as if they have a life of their own, without necessarily attending to their referents—and the ability to *contextualize*, to pause as needed during the manipulation process in order to probe into the referents for the symbols involved. Quantitative reasoning entails habits of creating a coherent representation of the problem at hand; considering the units involved; attending to the meaning of quantities, not just how to compute them; and knowing and flexibly using different properties of operations and objects.

3. Construct viable arguments and critique the reasoning of others.

Mathematically proficient students understand and use stated assumptions, definitions, and previously established results in constructing arguments. They make conjectures and build a logical progression of statements to explore the truth of their conjectures. They are able to analyze situations by breaking them into cases, and can recognize and use counterexamples. They justify their conclusions, communicate them to others, and respond to the arguments of others. They reason inductively about data, making plausible arguments that take into account the context from which the data arose. Mathematically proficient students are also able to compare the effectiveness of two plausible arguments, distinguish correct logic or reasoning from that which is flawed, and—if there is a flaw in an argument—explain what it is. Elementary students can construct arguments using concrete referents such as objects, drawings, diagrams, and actions. Such arguments can make sense and be correct, even though they are not generalized or made formal until later grades. Later, students learn to determine domains to which an argument applies. Students at all grades can listen or read the arguments of others, decide whether they make sense, and ask useful questions to clarify or improve the arguments.

4. Model with mathematics.

Mathematically proficient students can apply the mathematics they know to solve problems arising in everyday life, society, and the workplace. In early grades, this might be as simple as writing an addition equation to describe a situation. In middle grades, a student might apply proportional reasoning to plan a school event or analyze a problem in the community. By high school, a student might use geometry to solve a design problem or use a function to describe how one quantity of interest depends on another. Mathematically proficient students who can apply what they know are comfortable making assumptions and approximations to simplify a complicated situation, realizing that these may need revision later. They are able to identify important quantities in a practical situation and map their relationships using such tools as diagrams, two-way tables, graphs, flowcharts, and formulas. They can analyze those relationships mathematically to draw conclusions. They routinely interpret their mathematical results in the context of the situation and reflect on whether the results make sense, possibly improving the model if it has not served its purpose.

5. Use appropriate tools strategically.

Mathematically proficient students consider the available tools when solving a mathematical problem. These tools might include pencil and paper, concrete models, a ruler, a protractor, a calculator, a spreadsheet, a computer algebra system, a statistical package, or dynamic geometry software. Proficient students are sufficiently familiar with tools appropriate for their grade or course to make sound decisions about when each of these tools might be helpful, recognizing both the insight to be gained and their limitations. For example, mathematically proficient high school students analyze graphs of functions and solutions generated using a graphing calculator. They detect possible errors by strategically using estimation and other mathematical knowledge. When making mathematical models, they know that technology can enable them to visualize the results of varying assumptions, explore consequences, and compare predictions with data. Mathematically proficient students at various grade levels are able to identify relevant external mathematical resources, such as digital content located on a website, and use them to pose or solve problems. They are able to use technological tools to explore and deepen their understanding of concepts.

6. Attend to precision.

Mathematically proficient students try to communicate precisely to others. They try to use clear definitions in discussion with others and in their own reasoning. They state the meaning of the symbols they choose, including using the equal sign consistently and appropriately. They are careful about specifying units of measure, and labeling axes to clarify the correspondence with quantities in a problem. They calculate accurately and efficiently, express numerical answers with a degree of precision appropriate for the problem context. In the elementary grades, students give carefully formulated explanations to each other. By the time they reach high school, they have learned to examine claims and make explicit use of definitions.

7. Look for and make use of structure.

Mathematically proficient students look closely to discern a pattern or structure. Young students, for example, might notice that three and seven more is the same amount as seven and three more, or they may sort a collection of shapes according to how many sides the shapes have. Later, students will see 7×8 equals the well remembered $7 \times 5 + 7 \times 3$, in preparation for learning about the distributive property. In the expression $x^2 + 9x + 14$, older students can see the 14 as 2×7 and the 9 as $2 + 7$. They recognize the significance of an existing line in a geometric figure and can use the strategy of drawing an auxiliary line for solving problems. They also can step back for an overview and shift perspective. They can see complicated things, such as some algebraic expressions, as single objects or as being composed of several objects. For example, they can see $5 - 3(x - y)^2$ as 5 minus a positive number times a square and use that to realize that its value cannot be more than 5 for any real numbers x and y.

8. Look for and express regularity in repeated reasoning.

Mathematically proficient students notice if calculations are repeated, and look both for general methods and for shortcuts. Upper elementary students might notice when dividing 25 by 11 that they are repeating the same calculations over and over again, and conclude they have a repeating decimal. By paying attention to the calculation of slope as they repeatedly check whether points are on the line through $(1, 2)$ with slope 3, middle school students might abstract the equation $(y - 2)/(x - 1) = 3$. Noticing the regularity in the way terms cancel when expanding $(x - 1)(x + 1)$, $(x - 1)(x^2 + x + 1)$, and $(x - 1)(x^3 + x^2 + x + 1)$ might lead them to the general formula for the sum of a geometric series. As they work to solve a problem, mathematically proficient students maintain oversight of the process, while attending to the details. They continually evaluate the reasonableness of their intermediate results.

Connecting the Standards for Mathematical Practice to the Standards for Mathematical Content

The Standards for Mathematical Practice describe ways in which developing student practitioners of the discipline of mathematics increasingly ought to engage with the subject matter as they grow in mathematical maturity and expertise throughout the elementary, middle, and high school years. Designers of curricula, assessments, and professional development should all attend to the need to connect the mathematical practices to mathematical content in mathematics instruction. The Standards for Mathematical Content are a balanced combination of procedure and understanding. Expectations that begin with the word "understand" are often especially good opportunities to connect the practices to the content. Students who lack understanding of a topic may rely on procedures too heavily. Without a flexible base from which to work, they may be less likely to consider analogous problems, represent problems coherently, justify conclusions, apply the mathematics to practical situations, use technology mindfully to work with the mathematics, explain the mathematics accurately to other students, step back for an overview, or deviate from a known procedure to find a shortcut. In short, a lack of understanding effectively prevents a student from engaging in the mathematical practices. In this respect, those content standards which set an expectation of understanding are potential "points of intersection" between the Standards for Mathematical Content and the Standards for Mathematical Practice. These points of intersection are intended to be weighted toward central and generative concepts in the school mathematics curriculum that most merit the time, resources, innovative energies, and focus necessary to qualitatively improve the curriculum, instruction, assessment, professional development, and student achievement in mathematics.

Handout 4.5
Student Connections: Observing Students Playing Games

Select at least one of the games from Handout 4.3 to play with three groups of children. Write notes here about the strategies students use to play the game.

Name of game	
Group 1	
Group 2	
Group 3	

Session 5

Addition and Subtraction Word Problems (Part 1)

How do children make sense of addition and subtraction word problems?

Description

Word problems are the ideal starting place for developing students' understanding of addition and subtraction. When problems are based in familiar situations, students use the context of the problem to make sense of the mathematics. The structuring and wording of problems influence how children make sense of addition and subtraction situations.

Key Ideas

- Word problems enhance students' conceptual understanding of addition and subtraction.

- Young children understand and solve word problems in ways that are different from adults.

- Addition and subtraction word problems can be classified based on the structure and wording of the problem, rather than on the operation that might be used to solve it.

Outline of Activities

- 5.1 Examining "Simple" Word Problems   (20 minutes)
- 5.2 Discussing Student Reactions to Word Problems   (15 minutes)
- 5.3 Classifying Word Problems   (25 minutes)
- 5.4 Investigating Instructional Materials   (20 minutes)
- 5.5 Before the Next Session   (5 minutes)
- 5.6 Lesson Design Notes   (5 minutes)

What to Bring

- Instructional materials: addition or subtraction lessons
- Handout from previous session (Handout 4.4)
- Common Core State Standards: Standards for Mathematical Content

To Complete Before Session 6

- Student Connections: Word Problems I (Handout 5.5)

Facilitator Notes   Session 5

Addition and Subtraction Word Problems (Part 1)

If this is your first time facilitating the group, please refer to the more detailed facilitator guidelines in the Introduction. As the facilitator, it is generally your job to keep the conversation flowing and watch the clock. Use your judgment to decide when it's appropriate to extend a session for good conversation or when it's time to move on to the next activity. Remember to keep the group norms posted and revise them, as a group, as necessary.

Before the Session

- Make copies of the following handouts for each team member:
  - ☐ 5.1 Word Problems
  - ☐ 5.3 Classifying Problems by Difficulty
  - ☐ 5.4A Sample Lesson: Kindergarten
  - ☐ 5.4B Sample Lesson: First Grade
  - ☐ 5.4C Investigating Instructional Materials: Kindergarten Lesson
  - ☐ 5.4D Investigating Instructional Materials: First Grade Lesson
  - ☐ 5.4E Investigating Your Instructional Materials
  - ☐ 5.5 Student Connections: Word Problems I
- Gather the following materials to be used in this session:
  - ☐ Group norms (from Activity 1.4)
  - ☐ One or two pairs of scissors
  - ☐ Clear tape
- Remind team members to bring the following items from previous sessions:
  - ☐ Journal (and writing instruments)
  - ☐ Instructional materials: lesson on addition or subtraction
  - ☐ Handout 4.4 Common Core State Standards: Standards for Mathematical Content

During the Session

- Post group norms, and revise as a group as necessary.
- Activity 5.4: facilitate partnering, if necessary; serve as recorder of ideas.

After the Session

- Remind team members of homework, Handout 5.5 Student Connections: Word Problems I.
- Pass any team materials on to the next facilitator.

Activity 5.1 Examining "Simple" Word Problems

20 minutes   Handout 5.1 Word Problems

Word problems provide a strong foundation for students' conceptual understanding of addition and subtraction. When students encounter addition or subtraction problems based on familiar situations, they are able to use the context of the problems to make sense of mathematical relationships and to develop their own strategies for finding the answers. Although we often think of word problems as being more difficult to solve than basic arithmetic problems, the reverse is actually true. Research tells us that when children are learning to add and subtract, they benefit from simple and straightforward contexts that help them to conceptualize and model the situation (Carpenter et al., 1999; Kilpatrick, Swafford, & Findell, 2001; Van de Walle, 2009).

Because many word problems can be acted out or modeled with concrete objects or pictures, they offer students an entry point for reasoning about addition and subtraction situations and constructing solutions. However, as all experienced kindergarten and first grade teachers know, young children do not easily solve every word problem. While a student might be able to solve one word problem quite readily, the same student will likely struggle or even give up on another problem. Why is this? We will examine how the structure and wording of word problems influence the relative difficulty and way children typically solve them.

Read the word problems on Handout 5.1 and consider the context of the mathematical situation in each problem.

Cut apart and sort the word problems on Handout 5.1 into two groups: addition problems and subtraction problems.

Rank the problems in each group according to difficulty. That is, which addition problem(s) would your students find the easiest to solve? Which problem(s) would be the most challenging? Which one(s) would be "in between" or moderately difficult? Work individually on this task, and do the same for the subtraction problems.

Compare and discuss your rankings with your group.

- What factors did you consider when deciding your rankings?
- What features do the "easier" problems have in common?
- What features do the "challenging" problems have in common?
- Have you used word problems like these with your students?
- How might the contexts of the problems help students to find the solutions?

Record your sorting and rankings on the problem cards. Write + or – on each card to indicate whether it is an addition or subtraction problem. Write *E* for easy, *M* for moderate, and *C* for challenging. Save these problem cards for Activity 5.3.

Activity 5.2 Discussing Student Reactions to Word Problems

15 minutes

It is likely that problem card 3 from Handout 5.1 is one that you identified as a subtraction problem and ranked as a challenging problem.

> Tommy had 6 cars. His cousin gave him some more cars. Now Tommy has 8 cars. How many cars did his cousin give him?

Consider the following dialogue between a student who is struggling with this problem and his teacher:

Student: Teacher, I'm stuck. How do I do this problem?

Teacher: Do you think you should add or subtract to find the answer?

Student: I don't know. Is it a plus problem because the cousin gave him some cars?

Teacher: No, no. It's not adding. This is a subtraction problem. You see, you need to take 6 away from 8 because we don't know how many cars Tommy's cousin gave him.

Student: But the story says his cousin gave him some more. That means I should add.

Teacher: No, in this problem you need to subtract.

Discuss the dialogue with your group.

- Does this exchange sound familiar? Have you had the experience of talking with a student about a problem and the student seems to think very differently about the problem than you do? Relate a similar experience.

- What do you typically do in this situation?

- Have you talked with students about a problem and found that a child doesn't see the problem in terms of the operation that could be used to solve it? What have you done to overcome this mismatched communication? Would you suggest a different response for the teacher in the preceding dialogue?

Activity 5.3 Classifying Word Problems

25 minutes

Handout 5.3 Classifying Problems by Difficulty

Scissors

Clear tape

Researchers have studied young children's natural approach to solving word problems like the problems on Handout 5.1 and have confirmed that children indeed do not typically view word problems in terms of the operation that might be used to calculate an answer (Carpenter et al., 1999). Instead, children respond to the action or relationship in the problem and then consider the outcome of that action or relationship. Recall that the student represented in the dialogue in the last activity said, "But the story says his cousin gave him some more," which precluded him from thinking of this problem in terms of the operation of subtraction.

While adults and older children typically hear a word problem like this and automatically associate an operation with it, younger children naturally attend closely to the situation or story described in the problem. They use the action or relationships described in the problem as the basis for their reasoning about the solution. In order for teachers to respond to students' difficulty with certain problems, it is necessary for us to see these problems in the way that children do.

Return to the 10 cards you sorted in Activity 5.1. It was probably very easy for you to do the initial sorting in terms of the operation (addition or subtraction). Now you will re-sort these problems according to what researchers have identified as a young child's way of thinking.

Problem Category: Action

Some of the problems on the handout describe a situation that includes an action. An action problem describes a sequence over time that includes a beginning, a middle, and an end. In an action problem there is a starting quantity, a change to that quantity, and a resulting amount. The change involves either joining or separating sets of objects.

Problem Category: Relationships

Some of the problems on the handout do not describe an action, but rather describe a static relationship. In these problems, there is no time sequence for the information, no change over time, no beginning, middle, or end. Instead, these problems require the student to make sense of how quantities are related. The relationship involves either considering how parts relate to the whole set or making comparisons between sets.

Re-sort the word problem cards from Activity 5.1 into two groups: (1) problems that describe an action and (2) problems that describe a relationship. You should find that six of the problems are action problems and four of them are relationship problems.

Sort further within the action problems. Create two groups: (1) action problems that describe a *joining action* and (2) action problems that describe a *separating action*. Place these cards on Handout 5.3 in the appropriate sections of the grid. Look at the relationship problems and sort them further. Create two groups: (1) relationship problems that describe a *part-part-whole* relationship and (2) relationship problems that describe a *comparison*. Place these cards on Handout 5.3 in the appropriate sections of the grid.

Rank by difficulty. Place these problems in each section in order according to difficulty using the ranking you wrote in the last activity (*E* for easy, *M* for moderate, and *C* for challenging).

Compare and discuss the sorted problems and the difficulty rankings.

- Is there agreement among the group members about the problem categories? What questions or challenges, if any, did you have in sorting the problems?

- Where do you find the cards you marked with a + indicating an addition problem, and where do you find the cards you marked with a − indicating a subtraction problem in this sorting scheme?

- Which section(s) contain most of the problems identified as challenging?

- Return to the dialogue presented in Activity 5.2. With which problem type was this student struggling?

- Why might the student have struggled with the teacher's solution strategy relating the problem to subtraction?

As you may have discussed, *compare* problems are very challenging, especially for kindergarten and young first grade students. This is primarily because students in this age group are likely to compare groups of objects based on visual attributes (such as colors or which group takes up more space) rather than the number of objects included in the groups (Griffin, 2005). Students in kindergarten are learning how to compare and order numbers, as you examined in Session 4. Until they have an understanding of the sequence and magnitude of numbers, it is difficult for children to answer questions that ask them to determine *how many more* when comparing groups of objects.

In the next session, you will learn more about these research-based problem classifications. Leave the problem cards taped to Handout 5.3 and bring them to Session 6.

Activity 5.4 Investigating Instructional Materials

20 minutes

Handout 4.4 Common Core State Standards
Handout 5.4A Sample Lesson: Kindergarten
Handout 5.4B Sample Lesson: First Grade
Handout 5.4C Investigating Instructional Materials: Kindergarten Lesson
Handout 5.4D Investigating Instructional Materials: First Grade Lesson
Handout 5.4E Investigating Your Instructional Materials
Instructional materials: counting or subtraction lessons
Common Core State Standards: Standards for Mathematical Content

The goal in providing lessons or activities from different instructional programs is to give you a range of examples to consider when working on your prototype lesson. The sample lessons are not intended as exemplars, but rather are provided to demonstrate one way textbook authors have chosen to address the topic.

Review the sample lesson for your grade level on Handout 5.4A or 5.4B with a partner. **Try** some of the lesson activities. Look closely at the lesson and consider the following questions. Handouts 5.4C and 5.4D list the same questions in a table where you can record your responses.

- What big ideas, strategies, and mathematical models are being developed in the lesson (see Handout 2.3)?

- What are the important mathematical concepts underlying the lesson? How does the lesson reflect the concepts from the Common Core State Standards (see Handout 4.4 and Standards for Mathematical Content for your grade level)?

- What skills and knowledge are required to complete the tasks?

- For the kindergarten lesson, discuss the following questions:
  o What are the potential benefits of using 10 sticks?
  o Why show students how to organize groups of five? How could these numbers support understanding of place value and addition and subtraction?

- For the first grade lesson, discuss the following questions:
  o In activity 5.3, you sorted problems into two categories: action and relationship. In which category would you place the shark problems posed in this lesson?
  o Are the problems in this lesson easy, moderate, or challenging?

- What are the strengths of the lesson?

- What are some limitations, questions, and concerns that you have about the lesson?

Repeat the preceding process with a counting (kindergarten) or subtraction (first grade) lesson from your own curriculum. You can analyze the same lesson as a group or work individually on different lessons. Handout 5.4E has the same table as Handouts 5.4C and 5.4D and should be used to record your observations about the lesson from your curriculum.

Discuss the ideas recorded on the two handouts as a whole group.

Activity 5.5 Before the Next Session

5 minutes

Handout 5.3 Classifying Problems by Difficulty, with word problems from Handout 5.1

Handout 5.5 Student Connections: Word Problems I

Pose some of the word problems you sorted in this session on Handout 5.3 to your students. Pose at least one "easy" problem, one "moderate" problem, and one "challenging" problem. You should feel free to alter the values in the problems to appropriately meet students' needs, using smaller numbers for struggling students and larger numbers to find the limits of higher-achieving students. Again, the purpose of conducting the interviews is to find the mathematical limit for each of your students. Sit with students individually as they complete the tasks. Use Handout 5.5 to record the problems you choose, the problem types, and the difficulty rankings. There is also space to record your notes about how students solve the problems. Using your students' responses, be prepared to report in the next session whether you would like to change the difficulty ranking you had made for any of the problems.

Activity 5.6 Lesson Design Notes

5 minutes

The key ideas for this session are

- Word problems enhance students' conceptual understanding of addition and subtraction.

- Young children understand and solve word problems in ways that are different from adults.

- Addition and subtraction word problems can be classified based on the structure and wording of the problem rather than on the operation that might be used to solve it.

Reflect on what you learned during this session and how the ideas apply to each of the three themes in your Lesson Design Notes. A few prompts related to the themes follow. These are merely suggestions and should not limit your reflection or the ideas you capture.

- Where do you want to go?
  - In Activity 5.3, you examined addition and subtraction problem types. What types of word problems would you like your students to become proficient at solving?

- Where are you now?
  - In Activity 5.2, you discussed student reactions to word problems. What types of word problems do your students solve easily and which are challenging for them?

- What is the best way to get there?
  - In Activity 5.3, you investigated the relative difficulty of different problem types. How could this task inform the sequence of addition and subtraction lessons?
  - In Activity 5.4, you analyzed sample addition and subtraction lessons. What ideas from the sample lessons are you interested in trying out in your classroom?

References and Resources

Carpenter, T. P., Fennema, E., Franke, M. L., Levi, L., & Empson, S. B. (1999). *Children's mathematics: Cognitively guided instruction.* Portsmouth, NH: Heinemann.

Griffin, S. (2005). Fostering the development of whole number sense: Teaching mathematics in the primary grades. In M. S. Donovan & J. D. Bransford (Eds.), *How students learn: Mathematics in the classroom* (pp. 257–308). Washington, DC: National Academies Press.

Kilpatrick, J., Swafford, J., & Findell, B. (Eds.). (2001). *Adding it up: Helping children learn mathematics.* Washington, DC: National Academies Press.

Snider, A., & Burk, D. (2007a). *Bridges in mathematics: Grade 1, Teachers guide* (Vol. 1). Salem, OR: Math Learning Center.

Snider, A., & Burk, D. (2007b). *Bridges in mathematics: Grade K, Teachers guide* (Vol. 1). Salem, OR: Math Learning Center.

Van de Walle, J. A. (2009). *Elementary and middle school mathematics: Teaching developmentally* (7th ed.). Needham Heights, MA: Allyn & Bacon.

Handout 5.1
Word Problems

Cut these problems apart into 10 cards.

1 Sara had 5 sweaters. Her grandma gave her 3 more sweaters. How many sweaters does Sara have now?	**2** Milo has 2 dogs and 3 cats. How many pets does Milo have?	**3** Tommy had 6 cars. His cousin gave him some more cars. Now Tommy has 8 cars. How many cars did his cousin give him?
4 Carol had 7 books. She gave 3 of her books to her little sister. How many books does she have now?	**5** Matthew has 6 trucks: 2 are red and the rest are blue. How many blue trucks does Matthew have?	**6** Gabby had some pencils. She found 4 more pencils. Now she has 7 pencils. How many pencils did she have to start with?
7 Lily has 8 dolls and John has 3. How many more dolls does Lily have than John?	**8** Max had 8 trucks. Some of them broke. Now he has 3 trucks. How many trucks broke?	**9** Cassie has 7 balls. Eric has 2 more balls than Cassie. How many balls does Eric have?
10 Owen had some cookies. He ate 2 of the cookies. Now he has 6 cookies left. How many cookies did he have to start with?		

Handout 5.3
Classifying Problems by Difficulty

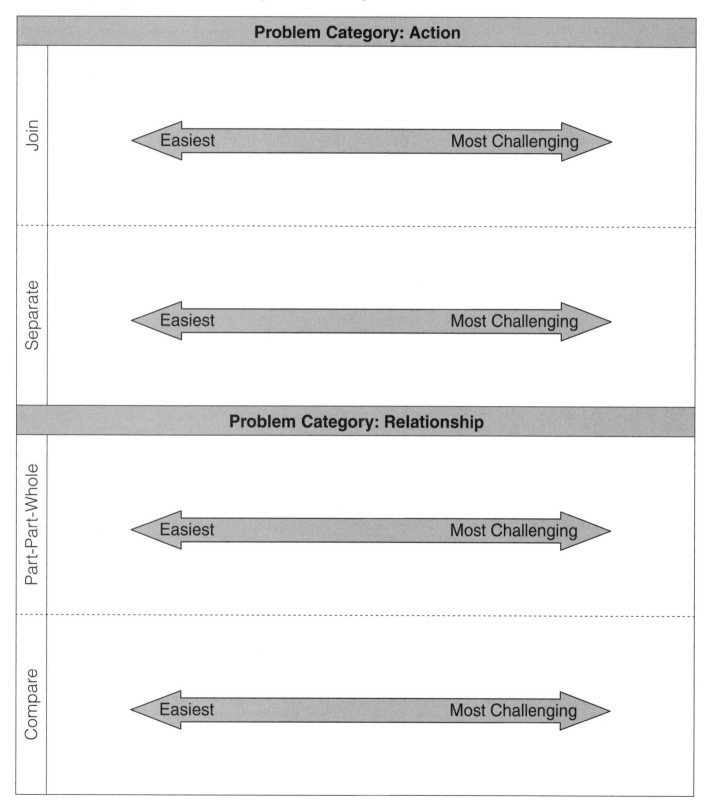

Sample Lesson: Kindergarten

Session 25

PROBLEMS & INVESTIGATIONS

Popsicle Stick Tallying

Overview

After children each count out 10 popsicle sticks, they create stick pictures for a few minutes. Then they learn how to set up their sticks in tally form, exploring various groupings and adding one at a time until they reach 10. After a quick stretch, they remove sticks from their collections 1 by 1, exploring various ways to determine the total number of remaining sticks as they work.

You'll need

★ 10 popsicle sticks for each child and 10 for yourself

★ 9″ × 12″ sheets of construction paper to serve as work mats (You'll need 1 for each child and 1 for yourself.)

★ Tally cards 1–10

Skills

★ adding 1's

★ subtracting 1's

★ counting forwards and backwards by 1's

★ instant recognition of quantities to 5

★ counting on from 5

Begin the session by setting out handfuls of popsicle sticks in various locations around the room. Ask each child to count out 10 sticks for him- or herself and join you in the discussion area. As children arrive with their sticks, have them sit in a circle or a U shape and give each of them a construction paper "work mat." Ask them to check their sticks once more to be sure they have 10. If someone has the wrong number of sticks, ask children around him or her to help make the needed corrections. Then give students a few minutes to explore with their popsicle sticks. Encourage them to make some stick pictures on their mats and then to look around at the things their classmates have made.

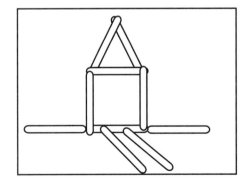

Finally, ask them to place their sticks above their mats. Once everyone is ready, have students set out 3 of their sticks on their mats, side by side. Model with your own sticks so each child will know what you mean. Can they change the quantity they have on their mat to 4 sticks? 2 sticks? (Keep an eye on children as they work at changing the quantities on their mats. Do they clear off all of their sticks and start again each time or do they add and subtract sticks easily?)

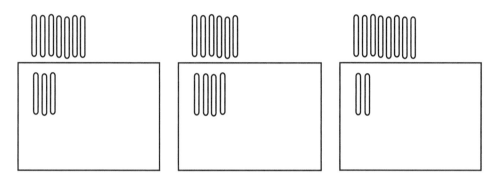

Ask them to change their group of 2 to 5 sticks and once they have that in place, show them how to pick up the fifth stick and set it diagonally across the four.

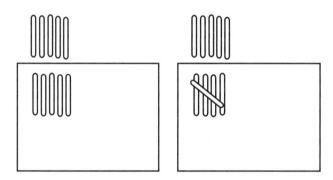

You might explain that organizing sticks in groups of 5 like this is called tallying, and that people use this method to make counting easier.

Can they add 1 more stick? How many do they have now? If they add 1 more, how many will they have altogether?

Continue in this manner until children have set up their second group of 5. Can they pick up the fifth stick and set it across the group of 4? How many do they have now?

You may want to have children stretch and wiggle for a moment before they begin to work backwards. Once they're ready to start again, ask them to take off the last stick they put on. How many sticks are left? How did they figure it out?

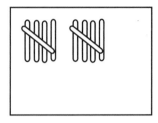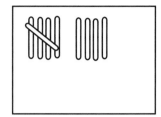

Teacher You took away 1 stick. How many do you have left?

Ella It's 9. I just know.

Randy Wait! 1, 2, 3, 4—this guy is 5, 6, 7, 8, 9. It's 9 all right.

Jonny You can see the 5. My mom and her friends write that when they play cards. She showed me. Then I can go 6, 7, 8, 9.

Leslie It's like the bugs. It's two 5's and then you take out 1 bug. 9 is just before 10 so I know it's 10.

Have children continue to subtract sticks one by one until they get back to zero. As with any "first time" challenge, some children will fall into these tasks with ease, while others will appear to be quite confused and perhaps prefer to play with the sticks instead of following along with the number tasks. To help children cooperate more fully with future tallying activities, it may help to have a small basket of the sticks available for free time over a few days. Trust that children who have had limited counting experiences before they came to school will be able to place and remove the sticks correctly with additional opportunities.

After the sticks have been collected, show children the tally cards, one at a time. Ask them to whisper to a friend how many sticks they see on each card and then ask for a volunteer to tell how many. Does everyone agree? How did they figure it out?

 Notes

■□ Bridges in Mathematics Tally Cards

■□ Bridges in Mathematics Tally Cards

■□ Bridges in Mathematics

Make 1 copy on cardstock. Cut apart on thin lines. Laminate.

Bridges in Mathematics Tally Cards

Bridges in Mathematics Tally Cards

Bridges in Mathematics

Make 1 copy on cardstock. Cut apart on thin lines. Laminate.

⬛ Bridges in Mathematics Tally Cards

⬛ Bridges in Mathematics Tally Cards

⬛ Bridges in Mathematics

Make 1 copy on cardstock. Cut apart on thin lines. Laminate.

Make 1 copy on cardstock. Cut apart on thin lines. Laminate.

■□ Bridges in Mathematics Tally Cards

■□ Bridges in Mathematics Tally Cards

■□ Bridges in Mathematics

Make 1 copy on cardstock. Cut apart on thin lines. Laminate.

Source: Authored by Donna Burk and Allyn Snider. Published by The Math Learning Center. Reprinted with permission.

Handout 5.4B
Sample Lesson: First Grade

Session 15

PROBLEMS & INVESTIGATIONS

Hungry Shark Subtraction

Overview

All the work children have done with crabs and sea stars in the past few days will lead to posing and solving story problems with 5's and 10's, but first we take a break to introduce some new Work Places. The first of these is Hungry Shark Subtraction, which features the "take away model" of subtraction. In the whole group version of this activity, the children get to be hungry sharks who gobble up fish crackers as the teacher tells subtraction story problems and records the action with pictures and number sentences. Next, the teacher shows a set of Hungry Shark Subtraction cards from the Work Place. Students make up subtraction stories to match each card and record the action, using pictures, numbers, and/or words. At the conclusion of the lesson, the teacher explains that children will find the Work Place version of Hungry Shark Subtraction in the collection tomorrow and sends them out to work on the current set.

Skills

★ exploring the operation of subtraction

★ recording the operation of subtraction

★ telling subtraction story problems

You'll need

★ fish crackers (enough for each child to have 20 crackers)

★ small cups or napkins (1 per child)

★ chart paper and markers or a white board and markers

★ Hungry Shark Subtraction cards (you'll need the 5's set)

★ individual chalkboards, chalk, and erasers

Work Places you'll need

2A Buttons Addition

2B Bugs in the Garden Addition

2C Spin & Write

2D Odd & Even

2E Pattern Block Patterns & Puzzles

2F Bugs in the House Subtraction

If you have an aide or parent volunteers, ask them to count out 20 fish crackers per child into small cups or onto napkins. If not, send children to wash their hands and pour crackers out onto napkins in several areas around the room. Have each child count out 20 for him- or herself from these piles. They can't eat them yet. Once they have their 20, they need to sit on the rug by the blackboard or chart paper.

When all of the children are gathered, explain that they will play the role of the hungry shark. Hopefully, with the bucket of Sea Animals, you have shared some books about sharks and children are aware of their role in the food chain. Though not every species of shark eats fish, many do. They will play the role of very hungry fish-eating sharks for this lesson. Begin the lesson with a simple subtraction story problem.

> 4 fish were swimming away from the school in which they had been traveling. The bubbles in the water caught the hungry shark's eye. She counted those fish—1, 2, 3, 4! She opened her mouth wide and managed to eat 2 of them. How many were left?

Teacher *How many fish did the shark see swimming together?*

Children *4!*

Teacher *When she opened her mouth, how many did she catch?*

Child *2. Those are really good fish. I like being the shark.*

Teacher *Are you telling me that 4 take away 2 leaves 2?*

Children *It's 2 all right. Can we eat the others?*

Teacher *No, those 2 remaining fish scurried back to find the other fish. Have yours join your other fish crackers.*

On chart paper or blackboard, show children how to write a number sentence to symbolize the story problem they just enacted. Then draw a picture to match.

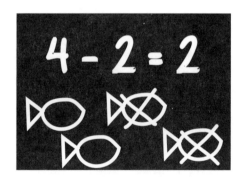

Continue with a few more story problems. As you pose each problem, stop and ask children how many the shark saw, how many the shark ate, and how many were left. Have the children guide you as you record each number sentence. What do the numbers and other symbols mean? How could you show each sentence with sketches?

> The hungry shark kept swimming and swimming. Like all sharks, he didn't have an air bladder. He had to keep moving or he would sink to the bottom. He was always hungry. Wait! What was that! 5 tasty fish were swimming nearby. He opened his mouth and gobbled up 4 of them. How many were left?

> The hungry shark was eager to find more fish to eat. She swam as fast as she could. Lo and behold! There were 6 fish in front of her. Thrashing through the water, she lunged at them and gobbled up 3. How many were left?

> The hungry shark began to swim more slowly. He hoped to sneak up on some fish so they wouldn't hear or see him coming. What luck! He saw 5 fish near some large seaweed. He opened his mouth wide and caught 4 of them. M-m-m good! How many were left?

> Her appetite was endless. All that swimming to keep from sinking to the bottom made her very hungry. She spotted 7 more fish. She swam slowly toward them. Suddenly, she opened her mouth wide. What luck! She managed to eat all 7. M-m-m good! How many were left?

Once the fish have all been eaten, get the children up for a stretch. Some will probably be quite thirsty, but they'll manage. Ask them to get chalkboards, chalk, and erasers and return to the discussion circle.

Then show students the set of Hungry Shark Subtraction cards that start with 5's. What do they notice?

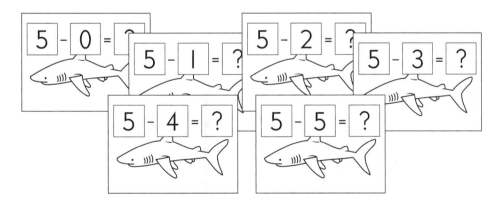

Children *There are sharks on those cards!*
I see numbers.
Those are the take-aways, like 5 take away 0 and 5 take away 1!
I know the answers on those!
The sharks have numbers on their fins!

Select one card and ask a volunteer to tell a story to match the number sentence on the card.

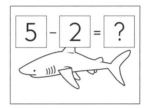

Then have children solve the problem on their chalkboards, using numbers, drawings, and/or words. As children find ways to show their thinking, call them up to the front of the group to show their work.

Will *I just wrote the numbers up to 5 and crossed out 2 of them for the fish the shark ate up. I crossed out the 4 and the 5, so it's easy to see that there are 3 left.*

Yannie *I drew 5 fish and circled the 2 that the shark gobbled up. There were 3 left. Then I wrote the numbers for this problem.*

Continue in this fashion with two or three more subtraction cards. Have children share their solution methods each time. Finally, explain that they'll find Hungry Shark Subtraction in the Work Places tomorrow.

 WORK PLACE NOTES

After the Hungry Shark lesson, have children put away their materials, collect their work folders and go out to Work Places. Remind them to mark their planning sheets each time they complete an activity and to store their papers in their work folders. Knowing that some of the current Work Places will soon be replaced by others, you might check through children's folders if you haven't already. Have they managed to get to at least half of the games and activities in the set? Do their planning sheets correspond to the papers in their folders, or are they forgetting to mark the stars and/or boxes as they complete tasks (or marking boxes too many times)? Are their papers done correctly, or are there mistakes that indicate that they either don't understand the tasks or don't understand the record sheets? Now that the Work Places have shifted almost completely into more structured tasks, many of which require paper work from the children, you might want to check their folders every few days. Work Places provide a perfect opportunity to meet with individuals or small groups of children who need extra instruction, and work sheets can often lead you to the students who need more help.

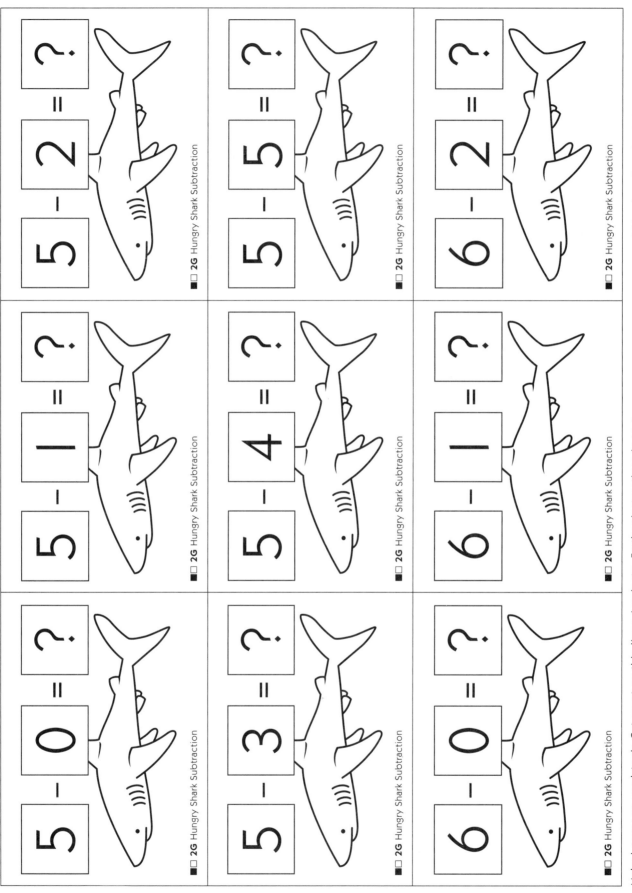

5 - 0 = ?
■ □ **2G** Hungry Shark Subtraction

5 - 1 = ?
■ □ **2G** Hungry Shark Subtraction

5 - 2 = ?
■ □ **2G** Hungry Shark Subtraction

5 - 3 = ?
■ □ **2G** Hungry Shark Subtraction

5 - 4 = ?
■ □ **2G** Hungry Shark Subtraction

5 - 5 = ?
■ □ **2G** Hungry Shark Subtraction

6 - 0 = ?
■ □ **2G** Hungry Shark Subtraction

6 - 1 = ?
■ □ **2G** Hungry Shark Subtraction

6 - 2 = ?
■ □ **2G** Hungry Shark Subtraction

Make 1 copy on cardstock. Cut apart on thin lines. Laminate. Further instructions in text.

Bridges in Mathematics, © The Math Learning Center

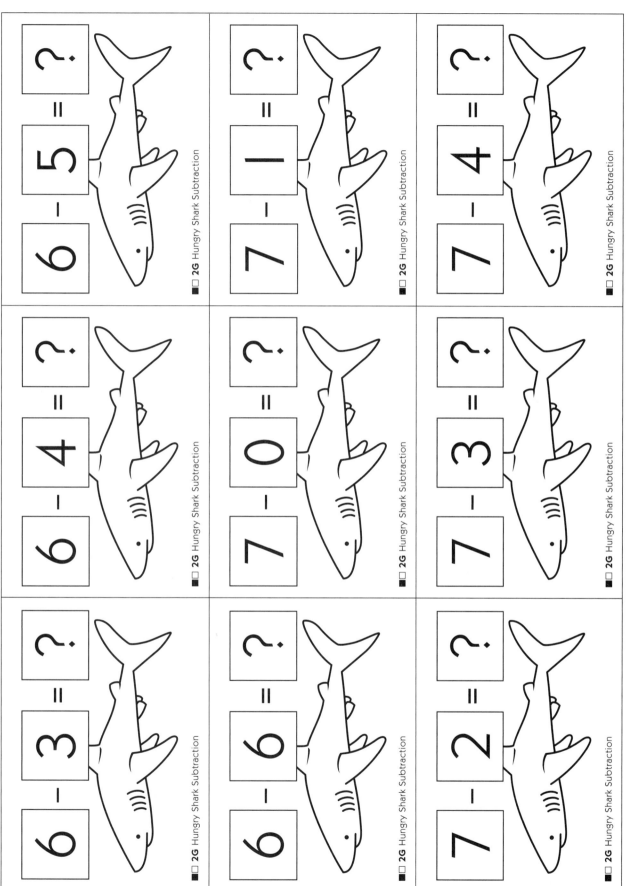

6 - 3 = ?

6 - 4 = ?

6 - 5 = ?

□ **2G** Hungry Shark Subtraction

□ **2G** Hungry Shark Subtraction

□ **2G** Hungry Shark Subtraction

6 - 6 = ?

7 - 0 = ?

7 - 1 = ?

□ **2G** Hungry Shark Subtraction

□ **2G** Hungry Shark Subtraction

□ **2G** Hungry Shark Subtraction

7 - 2 = ?

7 - 3 = ?

7 - 4 = ?

□ **2G** Hungry Shark Subtraction

□ **2G** Hungry Shark Subtraction

□ **2G** Hungry Shark Subtraction

Make 1 copy on cardstock. Cut apart on thin lines. Laminate. Further instructions in text.

Bridges in Mathematics, © The Math Learning Center

| 7 | – | 5 | = | ? |

■□ **2G** Hungry Shark Subtraction

| 7 | – | 6 | = | ? |

■□ **2G** Hungry Shark Subtraction

| 7 | – | 7 | = | ? |

■□ **2G** Hungry Shark Subtraction

Make I copy on cardstock. Cut apart on thin lines. Laminate. Further instructions in text.

Bridges in Mathematics, © The Math Learning Center

Source: Authored by Donna Burk and Allyn Snider. Published by The Math Learning Center. Reprinted with permission.

Handout 5.4C
Investigating Instructional Materials: Kindergarten Lesson

Lesson: *Bridges in Mathematics, Grade K, Teachers Guide* (Vol. 1), Math Learning Center (pp. 123–125).

Examine the lesson on Handout 5.4A and answer the following questions.

What big ideas, strategies, and mathematical models are being developed in this lesson?
What are the important mathematical concepts underlying the lesson?   **How does the lesson reflect the concepts from the Common Core State Standards?**
What skills and knowledge are required to complete the tasks?

What are the potential benefits of using 10 sticks?

Why show students how to organize groups of five? How could these numbers support understanding of place value and addition and subtraction?

What are the strengths of this lesson?	What are some limitations, questions, and concerns that you have about the lesson? What misunderstandings and difficulties might your students encounter?

Handout 5.4D

Investigating Instructional Materials: First Grade Lesson

Lesson: *Bridges in Mathematics, Grade 1, Teachers Guide* (Vol. 1), Math Learning Center (pp. 208–212).

Examine the lesson on Handout 5.4B and answer the following questions.

What big ideas, strategies, and mathematical models are being developed in this lesson?
What are the important mathematical concepts underlying the lesson? How does the lesson reflect the concepts from the Common Core State Standards?
What skills and knowledge are required for students to complete the tasks?

In Activity 5.3, you sorted problems into two categories: action and relationship. In which category would you place the shark problems posed in this lesson? Are the problems in this lesson easy, moderate, or challenging?

If you were to use this lesson, how would you adapt it to meet the needs of your students? Would you adjust the numbers, structure, wording, manipulatives, or context? How would these adjustments enhance students' conceptual understanding of addition and subtraction?

What are the strengths of this lesson?	What are some limitations, questions, and concerns that you have about the lesson?
	What misunderstandings and difficulties might your students encounter?

Handout 5.4E
Investigating Your Instructional Materials

Examine a lesson from your instructional materials that focuses on addition and subtraction concepts and answer the following questions. You will use your responses to develop the lesson in Session 12.

Lesson: Pages:

What big ideas, strategies, and mathematical models are being developed in this lesson?
What are the important mathematical concepts underlying the lesson? How does the lesson reflect the concepts from the Common Core State Standards?
What skills and knowledge are required for students to complete the tasks?

What are the similarities and differences between this lesson and the sample lesson from Handout 5.4A or 5.4B?	
What are the strengths of this lesson?	**What are some limitations, questions, and concerns that you have about the lesson?** **What misunderstandings and difficulties might your students encounter?**

Handout 5.5
Student Connections: Word Problems I

Use the problems sorted on Handout 5.3. The purpose of this activity is to collect information on the mathematical limit for each student, so adjust number values as needed. Provide counters, blank paper, and pencils. Allow students to use any method to solve these problems, and take notes here about the strategies they use to solve the problems.

Problem A			
Problem Type		Difficulty	
Student 1			
Student 2			
Student 3			
Problem B			
Problem Type		Difficulty	
Student 1			
Student 2			
Student 3			

Problem C			
Problem Type		Difficulty	
Student 1			
Student 2			
Student 3			
Problem D			
Problem Type		Difficulty	
Student 1			
Student 2			
Student 3			

Session **6**

Addition and Subtraction Word Problems (Part 2)

Why are some word problems more difficult for children to solve than others?

Description

Word problems are the ideal starting place for developing students' understanding of addition and subtraction. The structuring and wording of problems influence how children make sense of addition and subtraction situations. The relative difficulty of addition and subtraction problems is associated with the type of problem and the quantity that is unknown.

Key Ideas

- Both the category of the problem and location of the unknown quantity determine the relative difficulty of the different problems.
- Young children understand and solve word problems in ways that are different from adults.
- When teachers understand students' thinking about word problems, they facilitate more productive interactions about problems.
- Identifying characteristics of mathematical proficiency provides a framework for discussing the knowledge, skills, abilities, and beliefs that should be addressed in instruction.

Outline of Activities

- 6.1 Discussing Student Connections   (15 minutes)
- 6.2 Examining the Structure of Problems   (30 minutes)
- 6.3 The Problems With Word Problems   (15 minutes)

- 6.4 Defining Mathematical Proficiency   (20 minutes)
- 6.5 Before the Next Session   (5 minutes)
- 6.6 Lesson Design Notes   (5 minutes)

What to Bring

- Notes and student work: Student Connections activity (Handout 5.5)
- Handouts from previous sessions (Handout 5.3)

To Complete Before Session 7

- Student Connections: Word Problems II (Handout 6.5)

Facilitator Notes   Session 6

Addition and Subtraction Word Problems (Part 2)

If this is your first time facilitating the group, please refer to the more detailed facilitator guidelines in the Introduction. As the facilitator, it is generally your job to keep the conversation flowing and watch the clock. Use your judgment to decide when it's appropriate to extend a session for good conversation or when it's time to move on to the next activity. Remember to keep the group norms posted and revise them, as a group, as necessary.

Before the Session

- Make copies of the following handouts for each team member:
    - ☐ 6.2 Classifying Problems by Type
    - ☐ 6.4 Five Strands of Mathematical Proficiency
    - ☐ 6.5 Student Connections: Word Problems II
- Gather the following materials to be used in this session:
    - ☐ Group norms (from Activity 1.4)
    - ☐ Clear tape
    - ☐ Chart paper
    - ☐ Markers
- Remind team members to bring the following items from previous sessions:
    - ☐ Journal (and writing instruments)
    - ☐ Handout 5.3 (with 5.1 cards attached)
    - ☐ Completed homework, Handout 5.5 Student Connections: Word Problems I

During the Session

- Post group norms, and revise as a group as necessary.
- Activity 6.4: facilitate partnering, if necessary; serve as recorder of ideas.

After the Session

- Remind team members of homework, Handout 6.5 Student Connections: Word Problems II.
- Pass any team materials on to the next facilitator.

Activity 6.1 Discussing Student Connections

15 minutes   Handout 5.5 Word Problems I

One of your tasks from the previous session was to pose the problems from Handout 5.5 to your students. You were to pose at least one "easy" problem, one "moderate" problem, and one "challenging" problem.

Share results with your group:

- Which problem(s) did you identify as easy? Did your students find them easy to solve?

- Which problem(s) did you identify as moderate? Did your students struggle more with these problems?

- Which problem(s) did you identify as challenging? Were your students able to solve them?

- Based on your shared results, should you change any of your difficulty rankings? If so, change the letter (E, M, C) on the handout.

You will be analyzing and discussing student strategies for addition and subtraction in future sessions. Save Handout 5.5 for future discussions.

Activity 6.2 Examining the Structure of Problems

30 minutes   Handout 5.3 Classifying Problems by Difficulty (With Problem Cards)
                                     Handout 6.2 Classifying Problems by Type
                                                                Clear tape

In the previous session, you sorted addition and subtraction word problems based on the action or relationship in the problem. We will now consider additional differences between the problems and the relative difficulty each one presents for students.

Review the three action problems that involve a joining action (1, 3, and 6) and the three action problems that involve a separating action (4, 8, and 10). The distinguishing characteristic of an action problem is that it describes a sequence of action over time that includes a beginning, a middle, and an end. We call these problems *join* and *separate* problems (Carpenter et al., 1999; Van de Walle, 2009). In each of these action problems, the situation describes a starting quantity (a beginning), a change to that quantity (a middle), and a result (an end). What further distinguishes these problems from one another is which of these three elements is not known.

Is the resulting quantity unknown?	Result unknown
Is the change unknown?	Change unknown
Is the starting quantity unknown?	Start unknown

Place each of the joining action problem cards (1, 3, and 6) on Handout 6.2 in the appropriate spot. Do the same for the separating action problem cards (4, 8, and 10). (Tape the cards to hold them in place.)

Review the two problems that involve the relationship between parts of a whole set (2 and 5). The distinguishing characteristic of this type of problem is that it describes the relationship of part of a set to the whole set. What distinguishes these two problems from one another is which of these two elements is not known. We call these problems *part-part-whole* problems.

Is the whole set unknown?	Whole unknown
Is a part of the set unknown?	Part unknown

The remaining problems (7 and 9) describe situations that involve comparisons of two quantities. What distinguishes these two problems from one another is which of the elements is unknown. We call these problems *compare* problems.

Is the difference between the two sets unknown?	Difference unknown
Is the amount in the compared set unknown?	Compared set unknown

Place each of the remaining problem cards on Handout 6.2 in the appropriate spots. (Tape the cards to hold them in place.)

Researchers have studied students' responses to each of these types of problems and analyzed their relative difficulty for students. They have found that, in general, action problems in which the resulting amount is unknown are the easiest problems for students to solve. Problems in which the starting quantity is unknown are the most difficult, and problems where the change is the unknown quantity are moderately difficult for students. For part-part-whole problems, situations in which the whole is unknown are the easier problems for students to solve than ones in which a part of the set is unknown. Both comparison situations are usually very challenging for younger students, but problems in which the difference between two quantities is unknown are somewhat more accessible than ones in which the quantity in one set is unknown (Carpenter et al., 1999; Clements, 2004).

Kindergarten students tend to have difficulty with problem structures other than result or whole unknown. This is because they often do not know how to begin or how to plan out the steps they need to find a solution. Until students are able to make a plan and see the steps for finding a solution, they will have difficulty with the other problem types (Carpenter et al., 1999).

Even first graders typically find problems in which the change is unknown, or where the start is unknown, difficult because these problem types cannot be easily modeled (Van de Walle, 2009). When making sense of word problems, young children often act out or draw representations of the objects involved; however, if the starting amount or the amount that it is changed is not given in the problem, it is difficult to act out or draw a picture to represent the situation.

Compare and discuss your difficulty rankings with your team members.

- What difficulty ranking did you give each of the action problems?
- Do the researchers' conclusions about difficulty support your ranking?
- If not, what might account for the discrepancy?
- What new insights do you have about how students think about word problems based on Session 4 and Session 5?
- What questions do you have about problem types and the relative difficulty of problems?
- How might this information impact your instruction?

Write an open number sentence for each of the action problems (join and separate) that matches the time sequence in the problem. For example, the number sentence for problem 3 would be 6 + □ = 8 because the starting quantity is 6 cars, the amount of change is unknown, and the resulting amount is 8 cars. (Relationship problems are not as easily represented with number sentences.)

Reread this dialogue between a student struggling with problem 3 and the teacher (also presented in Session 5):

Student: Teacher, I'm stuck. How do I do this problem?

Teacher: Do you think you should add or subtract to find the answer?

Student: I don't know. Is it a plus problem because the cousin gave him some cars?

Teacher: No, no. It's not adding. This is a subtraction problem. You see, you need to take 6 away from 8 because we don't know how many cars Tommy's cousin gave him.

Student: But the story says his cousin gave him some more. That means I should add.

Teacher: No, in this problem you need to subtract.

Discuss how the problem structure classifications presented in this activity could help to explain the mismatched communication between the student and the teacher. How else might the teacher respond?

Activity 6.3 The Problems With Word Problems

15 minutes

Using word problems as a starting point to build students' understanding of addition and subtraction is the reverse order from a traditional approach to mathematics instruction. It may seem more logical to teach students how to compute with numbers first and save the "harder" word problems for later when children are more fluent with computation. Teachers often find that helping students solve word problems can be one of the most difficult aspects of teaching mathematics.

Discuss the following questions with your group:

- What are your thoughts about the placement of word problems in a learning sequence? Should they serve as a starting point or should we use them as an extension to learning addition and subtraction, after students develop computational fluency?

- Do you find it difficult to help students become successful with word problems? What makes this topic difficult to teach?

- Generate a list of some of the "problems" or challenges to helping your students become successful with word problems.

Researchers have done extensive work with teachers who use word problems to introduce and support student understanding of addition and subtraction. Consider the following (simulated) teacher-researcher exchanges:

Teacher: Word problems are too complicated for my students. They don't have strong reading skills yet and all the words just confuse them. They can barely handle the simplest problem like 3 plus 5; how can they possibly solve a problem with all kinds of details to keep track of?

Researcher: Word problems can and should be posed verbally to students so that reading ability will not be a factor. We often think of word problems as being more difficult to solve than basic arithmetic problems. The opposite is actually true. Problems that are posed in a familiar situation provide students an access point for solving them. Rich detail in a problem actually helps students because it allows them to make sense of the situation. When students can associate numerical quantities with particular items and actions in a story, they can make sense of what it means to add or subtract. When they are first learning how to add and subtract, students benefit from simple and straightforward contexts that help them to conceptualize and model the situations (Carpenter et al., 1999; Kilpatrick, Swafford, & Findell, 2001).

Teacher: I always found word problems to be the most difficult part of math, so I'm not sure that word problems are appropriate for my kindergarten and first grade students. I don't want my children to feel discouraged like I did, so I wait until they have developed confidence with number facts before posing word problems.

Researcher: While many adults struggled with word problems when they were learning math, this might be precisely because the word problems occurred at the end of a unit of study rather than being woven throughout. Research shows that we learn mathematics by making connections, and problem contexts help us to recognize these connections (Baroody & Standifer, 1993; Kilpatrick, Swafford, & Findell, 2001; Van de Walle, 2009). When word problems are the starting place, students can develop broad understanding of all types of addition and subtraction problems. Furthermore, word problems provide a context that helps children understand what to do in order to find the answer which leads to fluent computational ability. Developing computational fluency can be enhanced through work with word problems.

Teacher: I have to teach students all the clue words in order for them to be able to solve word problems. They need to know that *in all* means addition and *how many are left* means subtraction. It takes a long time to cover all of these phrases so that students can do these problems.

Researcher: Solving word problems should not be reduced to an exercise in pulling out the numbers and performing an operation. When teachers (or students) become focused on getting an answer as quickly as possible, they don't really read or listen to the problem. This is counterproductive. The great benefit of word problems is that they give the student the chance to build genuine understanding of mathematical operations. Students are deprived of this when instruction emphasizes looking for particular clue words or when instruction routinely includes only opportunities to solve the same type of problem over and over again. Solving many different types of problems helps students build a variety of strategies. It also helps them learn to reason about mathematical situations and develop flexibility in their thinking (Fuson, 2003).

Teacher: Teaching word problems is too time-consuming. I have a lot of content to cover and I need to make sure all of my students meet standards. If I spend too much time on word problems, I won't have time to teach them all the strategies and algorithms they need to know to move ahead.

Researcher: Children who learn mathematics through experiences with problems naturally develop strong problem solving skills. Without formal or direct instruction on specific number facts, algorithms, or procedures, children can construct their own solutions to a variety of word problems. Children can then understand the basic operations of addition and subtraction in terms of their own intuitive problem solving processes. Symbolic procedures and formal algorithms can be developed as extensions of students' intuitive solution processes (Carpenter et al., 1999; Cobb et al., 1991).

Discuss the following questions with your group:

- Which of these teacher concerns relates to a topic you discussed? What is your response to the researcher's comments?

- What problems did you list that were not addressed in these dialogues? How do you think one of these researchers might respond?

Write a response to the following question in your journal:

- What additional questions do you now have about using word problems to help students learn addition and subtraction?

Activity 6.4 Defining Mathematical Proficiency

20 minutes   Handout 6.4 Five Strands of Mathematical Proficiency

Now we will take an in-depth look at instructional goals. While we often think of goals in terms of specific concepts and processes to be accomplished in a single lesson, it is also helpful to step back and consider the bigger picture. Each lesson is a step in a journey that moves your students toward success in their mathematical careers. For this reason, when planning individual lessons, teachers should also be mindful of their long-term goals for their students. To define and discuss long-term mathematical goals we will consider what it means to be mathematically proficient.

Brainstorm individually in your journal about a student you have known whom you consider to be mathematically proficient. Write the name of that student at the top of the page. Now make a list of the qualities or characteristics that distinguish this child from others whom you do not consider to be as mathematically proficient. What could the proficient student do that others could not do?

- What kinds of things did the student say that revealed deep mathematical understanding?
- What were the visible attributes that led you to conclude that the student was mathematically proficient?

Also consider an adult that you have known whom you consider to be mathematically proficient. Add the qualities and characteristics of this person to your list.

- What has the adult said or done that makes you believe this individual is mathematically proficient?
- What are the visible attributes that led you to conclude that this adult was mathematically proficient?

Share your list with a partner. Identify four or five qualities or characteristics that you and your partner agree are important descriptions that apply to both adults and children who are mathematically proficient.

Share the four or five qualities you and your partner listed with the group. Keep a running group list on chart paper. If a quality is mentioned by more than one partner pair, put a star next to it.

Read Handout 6.4. This handout summarizes a definition of mathematical proficiency developed by the National Research Council (NRC). The NRC has described mathematical proficiency as being composed of five interconnected strands: conceptual understanding, procedural fluency, strategic competence, adaptive reasoning, and productive disposition.

Compare your group's statements recorded on the chart paper with the list on Handout 6.4.

- Which of the NRC strands are represented by qualities you have written on your list?
- Are there any statements on your chart paper that do not match any of the strands?
- Are there any strands for which you did not generate any statements?

Write in your journal about how the five strands relate to your students.

- Which of the five strands is strongly evident in many of your students? Name a few of these students.
- Which of the five strands is not particularly evident in many of your students? Why do you think this is so?

Activity 6.5 Before the Next Session

5 minutes   Handout 6.5 Student Connections: Word Problems II

Before the next session, observe three children as they solve several word problems on Handout 6.5. Your observations should include students of varied ability levels. As in previous data collection observations, adjust numbers in the problems as needed to help you determine your students' current mathematical limits. Remember that the purpose of this and other Student Connections activities is for you to collect some data about your students that will be shared at the next meeting. Sit with students individually as they each complete the tasks, and record what they say and do on Handout 6.5. Try to be as detailed as possible in describing how they approach the task, how difficult the task is for your students, what errors they make, and anything else of interest that happens during the interview.

Activity 6.6 Lesson Design Notes

5 minutes

The key ideas for this session are

- Both the category of the problem and location of the unknown quantity determine the relative difficulty of the different problems.
- Young children understand and solve word problems in ways that are different from adults.
- When teachers understand students' thinking about word problems, they facilitate more productive interactions about problems.
- Identifying characteristics of mathematical proficiency provides a framework for discussing the knowledge, skills, abilities, and beliefs that should be addressed in instruction.

Reflect on what you learned during this session and how the ideas apply to each of the three themes in your Lesson Design Notes. A few prompts related to the themes follow. These are merely suggestions and should not limit your reflection or the ideas you capture.

- Where do you want to go?
  - o In Activity 6.4, you discussed mathematical proficiency. Which of the five strands of mathematical proficiency would you like to explore further and help your students develop?
- Where are you now?
  - o In Activity 6.1, you shared and discussed the results of your student connections. Which problem types are your students able to solve easily? Which problem types are challenging? What is the range of numbers that your students are able to work with comfortably? What numbers are just beyond their reach?

- What is the best way to get there?
  - In Activity 6.2, you continued to investigate the relative difficulty of different problem types. How could this task inform the sequence of addition and subtraction lessons?
  - In Activity 6.3, you discussed the challenges of teaching word problems. Are there ideas or questions that came up during the discussion that could inform how you support students in solving word problems?

References and Resources

Baroody, A. J., & Standifer, D. J. (1993). Addition and subtraction in the primary grades. In R. J. Jensen (Ed.), *Research ideas for the classroom: Early childhood mathematics* (pp. 72–102). New York: Macmillan.

Carpenter, T. P., Fennema, E., Franke, M. L., Levi, L., & Empson, S. B. (1999). *Children's mathematics: Cognitively guided instruction.* Portsmouth, NH: Heinemann.

Clements, D. H. (2004). Major themes and recommendations. In D. H. Clements, J. Sarama, & A.-M. DiBiase (Eds.), *Engaging young children in mathematics: Standards for early childhood mathematics education* (pp. 7–72). Mahwah, NJ: Lawrence Erlbaum.

Cobb, P., Wood, T., Yackel, E., Nichills, J., Wheatley, G., Trigatti, B., & Perlwitz, M. (1991). Assessment of a problem-centered second-grade mathematics project. *Journal for Research in Mathematics Education, 22,* 3–29.

Fosnot, C. T., & Dolk, M. (2001). *Young mathematicians at work: Constructing number sense, addition, and subtraction.* Portsmouth, NH: Heinemann.

Fuson, K. C. (2003). Developing mathematical power in whole number operations. In. J. Kilpatrick, W. G. Martin, & D. Schifter (Eds.), *A research companion to* Principles and Standards for School Mathematics (pp. 68–94). Reston, VA: National Council of Teachers of Mathematics.

Griffin, S. (2005). Fostering the development of whole number sense: Teaching mathematics in the primary grades. In M. S. Donovan & J. D. Bransford (Eds.), *How students learn: Mathematics in the classroom* (pp. 257–308). Washington, DC: National Academies Press.

Kilpatrick, J., Swafford, J., & Findell, B. (Eds.). (2001). *Adding it up: Helping children learn mathematics.* Washington, DC: National Academies Press.

Van de Walle, J. A. (2009). *Elementary and middle school mathematics: Teaching developmentally* (7th ed.). Needham Heights, MA: Allyn & Bacon.

Handout 6.2

Classifying Problems by Type

	Problem Category: Action		
	Result Unknown	Change Unknown	Start Unknown
Join			
	Result Unknown	Change Unknown	Start Unknown
Separate			

	Problem Category: Relationship	
	Whole Unknown	Part Unknown
Part-Part-Whole		
	Difference Unknown	Compared Set Unknown
Compare		

Handout 6.4
Five Strands of Mathematical Proficiency

In the past, students in elementary school were considered successful when they had memorized procedures well enough to complete many simple problems in a short amount of time. The growing knowledge about how people learn makes it clear that memorizing procedures is not the same as learning mathematics with understanding and being able to think mathematically. Mathematical proficiency is the key to applying mathematics to unfamiliar and complex situations.

The National Research Council (as cited in Kilpatrick, Swafford, & Findell, 2001) has proposed a comprehensive definition of mathematical proficiency, made up of five components or strands. These five strands are intertwined, meaning that they are not developed in isolation but are interrelated.

1. *Conceptual understanding:* Mathematically proficient students understand mathematical concepts, operations, and relations. They know what mathematical symbols, diagrams, and procedures mean.

2. *Procedural fluency:* Mathematically proficient students carry out mathematical procedures—such as adding, subtracting, multiplying, and dividing numbers—flexibly, accurately, efficiently, and appropriately.

3. *Strategic competence:* Mathematically proficient students are able to formulate problems mathematically and to devise strategies for solving them by using concepts and procedures appropriately.

4. *Adaptive reasoning:* Mathematically proficient students use logic to explain and justify a solution to a problem or to extend from something known to something not yet known.

5. *Productive disposition:* Mathematically proficient students see mathematics as sensible, useful, and doable—*if* they are willing to work at it.

Handout 6.5

Student Connections: Word Problems II

Adjust the numbers in the problems to appropriately meet the needs of each student you are interviewing. The purpose of this activity is to collect information on the mathematical limit for each student. Provide counters, blank paper, and pencils for the students, and allow them to use any method to solve these problems. Write notes here about the strategies students use to solve these problems.

Problem A	*Jack had 9 markers. His mom gave him 7 more markers. How many markers does he have now?*
Student 1 Problem A	
Student 2 Problem A	
Student 3 Problem A	
Problem B	*Brianna has 5 pencils. Bret has 6 more pencils than Brianna. How many pencils does Bret have?*
Student 1 Problem B	
Student 2 Problem B	
Student 3 Problem B	

Problem C	There are 15 children on my soccer team. Six of them are boys and the rest are girls. How many girls are on my soccer team?
Student 1 Problem C	
Student 2 Problem C	
Student 3 Problem C	
Problem D	There were 12 apples on my tree. We picked 8 of them. Now how many apples are on my tree?
Student 1 Problem D	
Student 2 Problem D	
Student 3 Problem D	

Session 7

Children's Strategies: Direct Modeling

Overview

What strategies do students initially use to solve addition and subtraction problems?

Description

Given appropriate learning experiences and support, children will invent their own strategies for solving word problems. The progression that most students follow as they learn to solve addition and subtraction problems is one of the most well-understood aspects of mathematics learning. Direct modeling is the initial strategy that many children use to solve different types of addition and subtraction problems.

Key Ideas

- Children invent their own ways of solving mathematics problems, and understanding these strategies helps teachers to develop and support effective learning experiences.
- Solving mathematics problems using objects or pictures to stand for the items in the problem is a common strategy used by young children. This is called *direct modeling.*
- The limitations of direct modeling for solving more challenging problem types serve to encourage children to develop more efficient and sophisticated strategies.

Outline of Activities

- 7.1 Developing Word Problems   (15 minutes)
- 7.2 Defining Direct Modeling   (15 minutes)
- 7.3 Direct Modeling Strategies and Problem Types   (30 minutes)
- 7.4 Direct Modeling and the Development of New Strategies   (20 minutes)
- 7.5 Before the Next Session   (5 minutes)
- 7.6 Lesson Design Notes   (5 minutes)

What to Bring

- Notes and student work: Student Connections activity (Handout 6.5)
- Handouts from previous sessions (Handouts 6.2 and 6.4)

To Complete Before Session 8

- Investigating Instructional Materials activity for addition or subtraction models

Facilitator Notes   Session 7

Children's Strategies: Direct Modeling

If this is your first time facilitating the group, please refer to the more detailed facilitator guidelines in the Introduction. As the facilitator, it is generally your job to keep the conversation flowing and watch the clock. Use your judgment to decide when it's appropriate to extend a session for good conversation or when it's time to move on to the next activity. Remember to keep the group norms posted and revise them, as a group, as necessary.

Before the Session

- Make copies of the following handouts for each team member:
    - ☐ 7.1A Problem Types and Examples
    - ☐ 7.1B Developing Word Problems
    - ☐ 7.2 Problems to Classify
- Gather the following materials to be used in this session:
    - ☐ Group norms (from Activity 1.4)
    - ☐ Manipulatives (blocks or counters)
- Remind team members to bring the following items from previous sessions:
    - ☐ Journal (and writing instruments)
    - ☐ Handouts 6.2 and 6.4
    - ☐ Completed homework, Handout 5.5 Word Problems I and Handout 6.5 Word Problems II

During the Session

- Post group norms, and revise as a group as necessary.
- Activity 7.2: facilitate partnering, if necessary.
- Activity 7.3: facilitate partnering, if necessary.
- Activity 7.4: facilitate partnering, if necessary.

After the Session

- Remind team members of homework, Identifying Instructional Materials for addition or subtraction using models.
- Pass any team materials on to the next facilitator.

Activity 7.1 Developing Word Problems

15 minutes

Handout 6.4 Five Strands of Mathematical Proficiency
Handout 7.1A Problem Types and Examples
Handout 7.1B Developing Word Problems

Now that you have learned about the different types of problems, it is your turn to come up with some simple word problems for each type. The context of the problem should help your students to make sense of what they are being asked to do and suggest a way for them to model the problem.

In Session 5, you read what researchers say about the value of using familiar contexts for problems in order to enable students to make sense of situations and solve problems using invented and meaningful strategies. When children are provided problems that involve familiar situations, the context itself can provide an access point for solving them.

Review the problems types and the examples on Handout 7.1A.

Write two or three problems representing different problem types using familiar contexts for your students. Use Handout 7.1B to record your problems. Consider the following ideas for generating problems with meaningful contexts:

- Use events and students in your class.

- Use characters or settings from favorite stories.

- Use "famous" people (like the teacher, principal, physical education teachers, school custodian, etc.).

- Use national or world events (like the Olympics, an election, the Super Bowl or World Series, etc.).

Share the problems you have written. Discuss how they might be improved or edited to better fit the categories. Before the next session, you can complete your chart and make copies of your completed chart to share with your team. This way everyone will have a wealth of meaningful problems to use with students.

Discuss how the use of word problems set in familiar contexts could help students become mathematically proficient. How could the word problems you wrote support the development of each of the five strands?

1. Adaptive reasoning.

2. Strategic competence.

3. Conceptual understanding.

4. Productive disposition.

5. Procedural fluency.

Activity 7.2 Defining Direct Modeling

15 minutes   Handout 7.2 Problems to Classify

When children begin solving addition and subtraction word problems, they often use physical objects to represent the action or relationship described in the problems. The physical objects they use may be their fingers, blocks, or other small counters. They may also use a drawing to show the elements in the problem. The strategy of acting out or drawing to solve problems comes very naturally to children, even without any instruction or guidance from adults. This strategy serves as the basis for the later development of more efficient and sophisticated strategies.

Researchers have called the use of objects or pictures to represent every element in the problem *direct modeling* (Carpenter et al., 1999). The term refers to the fact that the student *models,* or acts out, the action or relationship in the problem using a physical representation. This label is potentially confusing because we often think of modeling as something that a teacher does and students repeat or replicate. However, direct modeling is a strategy that even very young students can use to solve problems without any teacher direction. The direct modeling *strategy* is also different from mathematical models as a domain of the learning landscape, which include physical, visual, and abstract ways to represent mathematical relationships and situations.

Discuss the following questions with your group:

- In your experience, have you observed kindergarteners and first graders using a direct modeling strategy, that is, using objects or pictures to solve a problem?

- Have you found it to be true, as the researchers suggest, that students will naturally use this strategy even without teacher direction or guidance? If not, why do you think this might be the case?

- What is your feeling about allowing students to use their fingers, objects, or pictures to solve problems? Is this a strategy that you encourage or discourage? Why?

In Session 6, you examined word problems and categorized them into different problem types based on the context of the problem and what is unknown in each. In this session, you will be exploring the strategies children typically use to solve word problems. The type of problem they are asked to solve influences their choice of which strategy to use.

Identify the problem type for each problem on Handout 7.2. Do this individually, using your notes from the last session as needed. Use the following shorthand to indicate the problem type:

JRU	Join–result unknown
JCU	Join–change unknown
JSU	Join–start unknown
SRU	Separate–result unknown
SCU	Separate–change unknown
SSU	Separate–start unknown
PPW-WU	Part-part-whole–whole unknown
PPW-PU	Part-part-whole–part unknown
CDU	Compare–difference unknown
CCSU	Compare–compared set unknown

Compare your work with a partner, and discuss any unresolved discrepancies with your group.

Activity 7.3 Direct Modeling Strategies and Problem Types

30 minutes

Handout 5.5 Student Connections: Word Problems I
Handout 6.5 Student Connections: Word Problems II
Handout 7.2 Problems to Classify

Children can use direct modeling to solve many, but not all, of the types of problems identified in Session 6. Although direct modeling is characterized by the use of objects or pictures to represent the action or relationship in a problem, it takes different forms based on the problem type. In the following vignettes, you will examine several instances of the use of direct modeling applied to various problems.

Use direct modeling to solve each of the problems on Handout 7.2. Simulate the approach of a kindergartener or first grader who does not know the answer and must rely on direct modeling to find the solution. You may find that it is easier to use direct modeling for some problems than for others.

- With a partner, use objects or pictures to solve each of the problems on Handout 7.2.
- Reflect on the process. Was direct modeling a straightforward process? Did you encounter any difficulty using direct modeling to solve this problem?

Share your experience and any difficulties you and your partner encountered with the whole group.

Read the following vignettes describing students solving some of the problems on Handout 7.2.

Problem: Mike had 9 pennies. His mom gave him 5 more pennies. How many pennies does Mike have now?

Vignette: Ricardo takes out 9 counting blocks, one at a time, saying "1, 2, 3, 4, 5, 6, 7, 8, 9" and links them into a chain of 9. Next, Ricardo takes out 5 more counting blocks, one at a time, saying "1, 2, 3, 4, 5" and links them into a chain. Then Ricardo links the two chains together and counts from one end, saying "1, 2, 3, 4, 5, 6, 7, 8, 9, 10, 11, 12, 13, 14. He has 14 pennies."

(First step)   (Second step)
"1, 2, 3, 4, 5, 6, 7, 8, 9"   "1, 2, 3, 4, 5"

(Third step)
"1, 2, 3, 4, 5, 6, 7, 8, 9   10, 11, 12, 13, 14"

Problem: Cassie has 3 crackers. Eric has 7 more crackers than Cassie. How many crackers does Eric have?

Vignette: Nina draws 3 squares on her paper, saying "1, 2, 3. That's what Cassie has. Eric needs 7 more . . . 1, 2, 3, 4, 5, 6, 7" as she draws 7 more squares. She says, "Eric has this many," indicating the whole collection. Now she counts all the squares. "Eric has 10 crackers."

(First step)   (Second step)

□ □ □   □ □ □ □ □ □ □

"1, 2, 3,   1, 2, 3, 4, 5, 6, 7"

(Third step)

"1, 2, 3,   4, 5, 6, 7, 8, 9,10"

Problem: My teacher had 12 erasers. She gave 7 erasers to her students. How many does she have now?

Vignette: Barry counts to 12, placing a block on the table with each count, saying "1, 2, 3, 4, 5, 6, 7, 8, 9, 10, 11, 12." He then counts from 1 to 7, removing a block with each count, saying "1, 2, 3, 4, 5, 6, 7." Then he counts the remaining blocks, saying "1, 2, 3, 4, 5. The teacher has 5 erasers left."

(First step: counting out 12 blocks)

"1, 2, 3, 4, 5, 6, 7, 8, 9, 10,11,12"

(Second step: removing 7 blocks)

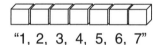

"1, 2, 3, 4, 5, 6, 7"

(Third step: counting remaining blocks)

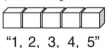

"1, 2, 3, 4, 5"

Problem: Haley had 6 cards. Paul gave her some more cards. Now she has 9 cards. How many cards did Paul give her?

Vignette: To solve the problem, Casey begins counting from 1 to 6, placing a cube on the table with each count and lining up the 6 cubes in a row. She begins to count again starting at 7, placing a cube on the table separate from the first 6 cubes; she stops counting at 9. Then she counts the number of cubes in the second group, saying "1, 2, 3. Paul gave her 3 cards."

(First step)   (Second step)   (Third step)

"1, 2, 3, 4, 5, 6,"   "7, 8, 9"   "1, 2, 3"

Problem: Michelle had 10 blocks. She gave some to her sister. Now she has 6 blocks. How many blocks did Michelle give her sister?

Vignette: Yan counted from 1 to 10, saying "1, 2, 3, 4, 5, 6, 7, 8, 9, 10," each time drawing a tally mark on his paper for a total of 10 tally marks. Then he crossed off 2 tallies. He counted how many he had left, saying "1, 2, 3, 4, 5, 6, 7, 8." He then crossed off 2 more marks and counted how many he had left, saying "1, 2, 3, 4, 5, 6." Finally he counted how many tally marks he had crossed off, saying "1, 2, 3, 4. Michelle gave 4 blocks to her sister."

Problem: Nate has 9 toy horses. Hannah has 16 toy horses. Hannah has how many more toy horses than Nate?

Vignette: Sophie takes out 9 counting blocks one at a time, saying "1, 2, 3, 4, 5, 6, 7, 8, 9," and then says, "These are Nate's." Next, she takes out 16 more counting blocks, saying "1, 2, 3, 4, 5, 6, 7, 8, 9, 10, 11, 12, 13, 14, 15, 16," and then says, "These are Hannah's." Next Sophie organizes Nate's blocks into a line. She then places one of Hannah's blocks on top of each of Nate's blocks. Finally she counts the unmatched blocks, saying "1, 2, 3, 4, 5, 6, 7. Hannah has 7 more than Nate."

(First step: counting out 9 blocks)

"1, 2, 3, 4, 5, 6, 7, 8, 9"

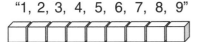

(Second step: counting out 16 blocks)

"1, 2, 3, 4, 5, 6, 7, 8, 9, 10,11,12,13,14,15,16"

(Third step: lining up blocks from both sets and counting unmatched blocks)

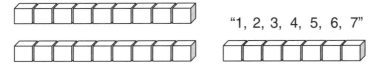

"1, 2, 3, 4, 5, 6, 7"

Discuss the following questions with your group:

- What are the common features in each of the strategies described in these vignettes? What are some variations or subtle differences between some of them?

- Review the Student Connections activities from Session 5 and Session 6 (Handouts 5.5 and 6.5). Did your students use direct modeling strategies similar to the ones described in these vignettes? Save your notes about your students' strategies for further reference as we review additional strategies.

- Review the components of a learning landscape on Handout 2.3. What strategies have you listed so far? Are there strategies that you would like to add to the landscape based on today's session?

Activity 7.4 Direct Modeling and the Development of New Strategies

20 minutes

Use direct modeling to solve the *join–start unknown* and *separate–start unknown* problems on Handout 7.2 (problems 8 and 10, for which there were no vignettes). Simulate the actions of a student who does not know the answer and must rely on direct modeling to find the solution.

- With a partner, use objects or pictures to solve the *join–start unknown* problem on Handout 7.2. Reflect on the process. Was this a straightforward process? How did you represent each quantity in the problem? Did you encounter any difficulty using direct modeling to solve this problem?

- With a partner, use objects or pictures to solve the *separate–start unknown* problem on Handout 7.2. Reflect on the process. Was this a straightforward process? How did you represent each quantity in the problem? Did you encounter any difficulty using direct modeling to solve this problem?

As you probably noticed while using direct modeling to solve these two problems, it is difficult to do. Because the starting amount is unknown, children who use direct modeling really have only one way to approach this kind of problem. They must use trial and error. They make a guess for the starting amount, act out the problem, and then see if they end with the correct amount. If not, they must make a new starting guess and try again. Using direct modeling to solve *join–start unknown* and *separate–start unknown* problems is not an efficient strategy, and students who rely solely on direct modeling will often give up or not even attempt these kinds of problems.

Keep in mind that direct modeling is only one type of strategy. There are other more efficient and more sophisticated ways to solve word problems. It should be the teacher's instructional goal to help all children develop a repertoire of strategies that they can flexibly apply depending on the complexity of the problem. In Sessions 8, 9, and 10, we will review the next two levels of strategies and consider how children apply them to various types of problems.

Discuss the following questions with your group:

- Researchers have identified direct modeling as the most basic strategy that virtually all children can use to solve problems (Carpenter et al., 1999). In your experience, have you found this to be true? Have you encountered children who have seemed unable to directly model problems? If so, why do you think they have struggled?

- Research also tells us that children naturally progress from direct modeling to more efficient strategies for solving problems, without instruction or guidance from adults. Has this been your experience? Have you observed students using their own ways of solving problems? What kinds of classroom experiences contribute to this kind of student-invented strategy?

- Direct modeling has its limitations when applied to more challenging problems like start unknown problems. Should teachers pose challenging problems like these to students who rely on direct modeling? What do you see as the advantages and disadvantages?

Activity 7.5 Before the Next Session

5 minutes

Instructional Materials: Models for Addition or Subtraction

In Session 8, you will be analyzing lessons that address models for addition and subtraction, specifically lessons that use the number line as a model. Between now and the next session, identify an addition or subtraction lesson from your instructional materials that uses at least one model. You might select a lesson that you have not taught before, one that you particularly enjoy teaching, or one that is challenging to teach.

The activity in Session 8 will focus on the following questions:

- What big ideas, strategies, and mathematical models are being developed in the lesson?
- What skills and knowledge are required to complete the tasks?
- What are the important mathematical concepts underlying the lesson?
- What are the strengths of the lesson?
- What are some limitations, questions, and concerns that you have about the lesson?

Activity 7.6 Lesson Design Notes

5 minutes

The key ideas for this session are

- Children invent their own ways of solving mathematics problems, and understanding these strategies helps teachers to develop and support effective learning experiences.
- Solving mathematics problems using objects or pictures to stand for the items in the problem is a common strategy used by young children. This is called *direct modeling*.
- The limitations of direct modeling for solving more challenging problem types serve to encourage children to develop more efficient and sophisticated strategies.

Reflect on what you learned during this session and how the ideas apply to each of the three themes in your Lesson Design Notes. A few prompts related to the themes follow. These are merely suggestions and should not limit your reflection or the ideas you capture.

- Where do you want to go?
  o In Activity 7.4, it states that "research tells us that children naturally progress from direct modeling to more efficient strategies for solving problems." What might "more efficient strategies for solving problems" look like or sound like? Do any of your students use these more efficient strategies yet?
- Where are you now?
  o In Activities 7.2 and 7.3, you examined the strategy of direct modeling. What did you learn that helps you identify where your students are in their understanding of addition and subtraction?

- What is the best way to get there?
  - In Activity 7.1, you developed word problems. What considerations did you make in writing word problems for your students?
  - What instructional strategies will you use to support students who use direct modeling to solve addition and subtraction problems?
  - What ideas came up in your discussion about lessons on word problems that support the development of mathematical proficiency?

References and Resources

Carpenter, T. P., Fennema, E., Franke, M. L., Levi, L., & Empson, S. B. (1999). *Children's mathematics: Cognitively guided instruction.* Portsmouth, NH: Heinemann.

Fosnot, C. T., & Dolk, M. (2001). *Young mathematicians at work: Constructing number sense, addition, and subtraction.* Portsmouth, NH: Heinemann.

Fuson, K. C. (2004). Pre-K to Grade 2 goals and standards: Achieving 21st century mastery for all. In D. H. Clements, J. Sarama, & A.-M. DiBiase (Eds.), *Engaging young children in mathematics: Standards for early childhood mathematics education* (pp. 105–148). Mahwah, NJ: Lawrence Erlbaum.

Kilpatrick, J., Swafford, J., & Findell, B. (Eds.). (2001). *Adding it up: Helping children learn mathematics.* Washington, DC: National Academies Press.

Handout 7.1A

Problem Types and Examples

<table>
<tr><td rowspan="5">Action problems</td><td colspan="3" align="center">Join</td></tr>
<tr><td align="center">Result Unknown</td><td align="center">Change Unknown</td><td align="center">Start Unknown</td></tr>
<tr><td>Sara had 5 sweaters. Her grandma gave her 3 more sweaters. How many sweaters does Sara have now?</td><td>Sara had 5 sweaters. Her grandma gave her some more sweaters. Now she has 8 sweaters. How many sweaters did Sara's grandma give her?</td><td>Sara had some sweaters. Her grandma gave her 3 more sweaters. Now she has 8 sweaters. How many sweaters did Sara have to begin with?</td></tr>
<tr><td colspan="3" align="center">Separate</td></tr>
<tr><td>

Result Unknown

Carol had 7 books. She gave 3 of her books to her little sister. How many books does she have now?</td><td>

Change Unknown

Carol had 7 books. She gave some of her books to her little sister. Now she has 4 books. How many books did she give away?</td><td>

Start Unknown

Carol had some books. She gave 3 of her books to her little sister. Now she has 4 books. How many books did she have to begin with?</td></tr>
<tr><td rowspan="5">Relationship problems</td><td colspan="3" align="center">Part-Part-Whole</td></tr>
<tr><td align="center">Whole Unknown</td><td align="center">Part Unknown</td><td></td></tr>
<tr><td>Milo has 2 blue trucks and 3 red trucks. How many trucks does Milo have?</td><td>Milo has 5 trucks: 2 of the trucks are blue and the rest are red. How many red trucks does Milo have?</td><td></td></tr>
<tr><td colspan="3" align="center">Compare</td></tr>
<tr><td>

Difference Unknown

Matt has 6 cats. Shelley has 2 cats. How many more cats does Matt have than Shelley?</td><td>

Set (Compared Set) Unknown

Shelley has 2 cats. Matt has 4 more cats than Shelley. How many cats does Matt have?</td><td>

Set (Referent) Unknown

Matt has 6 cats. He has 4 more cats than Shelley. How many cats does Shelley have?</td></tr>
</table>

Handout 7.1B
Developing Word Problems

	Problem Category: Action		
	Result Unknown	Change Unknown	Start Unknown
Join			
	Result Unknown	Change Unknown	Start Unknown
Separate			

	Problem Category: Relationship	
	Whole Unknown	Part Unknown
Part-Part-Whole		
	Difference Unknown	Compared Set Unknown
Compare		

Handout 7.2

Problems to Classify

	Problem Type	Sample Problem
1		Michelle had 10 blocks. She gave some to her sister. Now she has 6 blocks. How many blocks did Michelle give her sister?
2		Cassie has 3 crackers. Eric has 7 more crackers than Cassie. How many crackers does Eric have?
3		Milo has 11 pencils. He has 6 that are sharpened and the rest are not sharpened. How many unsharpened pencils does Milo have?
4		Haley had 6 cards. Paul gave her some more cards. Now she has 9 cards. How many cards did Paul give her?
5		My teacher had 12 erasers. She gave 7 erasers to her students. How many erasers does she have now?
6		Eduardo has 3 pennies and 4 nickels. How many coins does Eduardo have?
7		Mike had 9 pennies. His mom gave him 5 more pennies. How many pennies does Mike have now?
8		Angelica had some stickers. She gave 9 of her stickers to her friend. Now she has 4 stickers. How many stickers did she have to begin with?
9		Nate has 9 toy horses. Hannah has 16 toy horses. Hannah has how many more toy horses than Nate?
10		Oliver had some presents. His aunt gave him 4 more presents. Now he has 13 presents. How many presents did Oliver have to begin with?

Session 8

Children's Strategies: Counting Strategies

Overview

What strategies do students develop next in the learning progression for solving addition and subtraction problems?

Description

The progression that most students follow as they develop increasingly sophisticated strategies for solving problems is one of the most well-understood aspects of mathematics learning. Understanding the progression from direct modeling to various counting strategies for solving addition and subtraction problems helps teachers to create effective learning experiences.

Key Ideas

- Children invent their own ways of solving mathematics problems, and understanding these strategies helps teachers to develop and support effective learning experiences.

- Solving problems using counting strategies is a natural progression from direct modeling and is a more efficient step requiring a level of abstract thinking.

- *Counting on* and *counting down* are two kinds of counting strategies.

Outline of Activities

- 8.1 Defining Counting Strategies   (15 minutes)
- 8.2 Counting Strategies and Problem Types   (20 minutes)
- 8.3 Investigating Instructional Materials   (25 minutes)
- 8.4 More About Counting Strategies   (20 minutes)
- 8.5 Before the Next Session   (5 minutes)
- 8.6 Lesson Design Notes   (5 minutes)

What to Bring

- Instructional materials from a lesson using models for addition or subtraction.
- Handouts from previous sessions (Handouts 4.4, 5.5, 6.5, 7.1B, and 7.2)
- Common Core State Standards: Standards for Mathematical Content

To Complete Before Session 9

- Student Connections: Word Problems III (Handout 8.5)

Facilitator Notes   Session 8

Children's Strategies: Counting Strategies

If this is your first time facilitating the group, please refer to the more detailed facilitator guidelines in the Introduction. As the facilitator, it is generally your job to keep the conversation flowing and watch the clock. Use your judgment to decide when it's appropriate to extend a session for good conversation or when it's time to move on to the next activity. Remember to keep the group norms posted and revise them, as a group, as necessary.

Before the Session

- Make copies of the following handouts for each team member:
    - ☐ 8.3A Sample Lesson: Kindergarten
    - ☐ 8.3B Sample Lesson: First Grade
    - ☐ 8.3C Investigating Instructional Materials: Kindergarten Lesson
    - ☐ 8.3D Investigating Instructional Materials: First Grade Lesson
    - ☐ 8.3E Investigating Your Instructional Materials
    - ☐ 8.4 Counting Strategies
    - ☐ 8.5 Student Connections: Word Problems III
- Gather the following materials to be used in this session:
    - ☐ Group norms (from Activity 1.4)
- Remind team members to bring the following items from previous sessions:
    - ☐ Journal (and writing instruments)
    - ☐ Handouts 4.4, 5.5, 6.5, 7.1B, and 7.2
    - ☐ Common Core State Standards: Standards for Mathematical Content
    - ☐ Instructional materials: lesson using models for addition or subtraction

During the Session

- Post group norms, and revise as a group as necessary.

After the Session

- Remind team members of homework, Handout 8.5 Student Connections: Word Problems III
- Pass any team materials on to the next facilitator.

Activity 8.1 Defining Counting Strategies

15 minutes

After students become confident solving many problem types using direct modeling strategies, there is a natural progression to another type of strategy that does not require the student to build or draw all elements of a problem. Strategies that involve students holding some number values in their heads and then *counting on* or *counting back* to find solutions are the natural next steps for students.

The label "counting" is potentially confusing because, as we have seen in previous examples, students count when they are using direct modeling to solve a problem. It is also possible for students to use objects, fingers, or pictures when using a counting strategy. The distinguishing characteristic that identifies a strategy as a *counting strategy* is that a student does not need to build or draw all quantities in the problem, but can abstractly keep track of one of the quantities without building or drawing it. This distinction should become clearer as you read and discuss the vignettes in the following activities.

As children become more familiar with solving a wide variety of problems and working with numbers, they naturally move from direct modeling to counting strategies. Children no longer need to use models to represent each object in the problem because they are able to see numbers as abstract units and use the counting sequence to find an answer (Carpenter et al., 1999).

Discuss the following questions with your group:

- Have you found it to be true, as the researchers suggest, that students will naturally use counting strategies, even without teacher direction or guidance? If not, why do you think this is so?

- Have your ideas about allowing students to count on their fingers changed as you have worked through the past sessions? If so, why?

Activity 8.2 Counting Strategies and Problem Types

20 minutes

Handout 5.5 Student Connections: Word Problems I
Handout 6.5 Student Connections: Word Problems II
Handout 7.2 Problems to Classify

Like direct modeling, counting strategies take different forms based on the problem type. Some problems lend themselves to solutions by counting better than others. As you will see in the following vignettes, even when children use a counting strategy, there are variations in the use of this strategy depending on the child and on the type of problem.

Read the following vignettes describing students solving problems on Handout 7.2.

Problem: Mike had 9 pennies. His mom gave him 5 more pennies. How many pennies does Mike have now?

Vignette: To solve the problem, Chloe says 9, then pauses and counts, "10, 11, 12, 13, 14." Chloe extends 1 finger with each count beginning with 10. When she extends 5 fingers, she stops counting and says, "He has 14 pennies."

"9 . . . 10, 11, 12, 13, 14"

Problem: Eduardo has 4 nickels and 3 pennies. How many coins does Eduardo have?

Vignette: Jenna makes 3 tally marks on the page saying a number with each tally, counting "1, 2, 3," and then says, "That's the pennies." Next, she says, "Okay, there are 4 nickels so . . . 4" and pauses. Without making any more tallies, she continues the count from 4, tapping the original tally marks with each count, saying "5, 6, 7." She says, "He has 7 coins."

1 2 3
| | |
"4 . . .   5, 6, 7"

Problem: Cassie has 3 crackers. Eric has 7 more crackers than Cassie. How many crackers does Eric have?

Vignette: Brett says, "I'll start with 7 because it will be easier." He says 7 then pauses. Next he places a cube on the table for each count saying "8, 9, 10." Brett says, "Eric has 10 crackers."

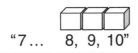

"7 . . .   8, 9, 10"

Problem: My teacher had 12 erasers. She gave 7 erasers to her students. How many does she have now?

Vignette: Sarah says 12, then she counts back from 12, extending a finger with each count and stopping after she has 7 fingers extended, saying "11, 10, 9, 8, 7, 6, 5. She has 5 erasers left."

"12 . . . 11, 10, 9, 8, 7, 6, 5"

Problem: Nate has 9 toy horses. Hannah has 16 toy horses. Hannah has how many more toy horses than Nate?

Vignette: Tim says 16 and makes a tally, saying a number with each tally, and stopping at 9, "15, 14, 13, 12, 11, 10, 9." Finally he counts his tallies. "Nate has 7 less than Hannah."

$$| \quad | \quad | \quad | \quad | \quad | \quad |$$
"16... 15 14 13 12 11 10 9"
"1 2 3 4 5 6 7"

Discuss the following questions with your group:

- What are the common features in each of the strategies described in these vignettes? What are some variations or subtle differences between some of them?

- Refer back to the direct modeling vignettes in Session 7. How are counting strategies different from direct modeling strategies? How is counting more efficient than direct modeling?

- What are some similarities between counting strategies and direct modeling strategies?

- Review the Student Connections activities from previous sessions (Handouts 5.5, 6.5, and 7.5). Did your students use counting strategies similar to the ones described in these vignettes? Save your notes about your students' strategies for further reference as we review additional strategies.

Activity 8.3 Investigating Instructional Materials

25 minutes

Handout 4.4 Common Core State Standards
Handout 8.3A Sample Lesson: Kindergarten
Handout 8.3B Sample Lesson: First Grade
Handout 8.3C Investigating Instructional Materials: Kindergarten Lesson
Handout 8.3D Investigating Instructional Materials: First Grade Lesson
Handout 8.3E Investigating Your Instructional Materials
Instructional materials: models for addition and subtraction
Common Core State Standards: Standards for Mathematical Content

The goal in providing lessons or activities from different instructional programs is to give you a range of examples to consider when working on your prototype lesson. The sample lessons are not intended as exemplars, but rather are provided to demonstrate one way textbook authors have chosen to address the topic.

Review the sample activity for your grade level on Handout 8.3A or 8.3B with a partner, and try some of the lesson activities. Look closely at the lesson and consider the following questions. Handouts 8.3C and 8.3D list the same questions in a table where you can record your responses.

- What big ideas, strategies, and mathematical models are being developed in the lesson (see Handout 2.3 in your journal)?

- What are the important mathematical concepts underlying the lesson? How does the lesson reflect the concepts from the Common Core State Standards (see Handout 4.4 and Standards for Mathematical Content for your grade level)?
- What skills and knowledge are required to complete the tasks?
- What strands of mathematical proficiency are represented in the lesson?
- For the kindergarten lesson, discuss the following questions:
  - The lesson suggests reading a book about counting back, acting out the problem with students, and creating a drawing on the board to represent the story and action of subtraction. How does each of these help students build strategies for solving word problems?
  - The lesson suggests that pairs of students solve the story problem. What opportunities for learning are provided for students who work together? What are some of the challenges that you have had with pairs of students working together?
  - The lesson suggests that students connect nine links and then count back as they remove one link at a time. How does this support students in using a counting strategy?
- For the first grade lesson, discuss the following questions:
  - How does this lesson support students' use of counting strategies? How does the use of the number line encourage students' use of counting strategies? How might the use of counters or cubes, instead of the number line, influence the strategies used by students?
  - How does the selection of adding 0, 1, or 2 encourage the use of counting strategies?
  - How might the lesson and the use of the number line be adapted for other problem types?
- What are the strengths of the lesson?
- What are some limitations, questions, and concerns that you have about the lesson?

Repeat the preceding process with a lesson from your own curriculum. If possible, select a lesson for analysis that focuses on the same topic or concepts as the sample lesson. You can analyze the same lesson as a group or work individually on different lessons. Handout 8.3E has the same table as Handouts 8.3C and 8.3D and should be used to record your observations about the lesson from your curriculum.

Discuss the ideas recorded on the two handouts as a whole group.

Activity 8.4 More About Counting Strategies

20 minutes   Handout 8.4 Counting Strategies

In this session, you looked at how counting strategies apply to 5 of the 10 problem types. However, counting strategies can be applied to the other problem types.

Review the descriptions of strategies and associated problem types on Handout 8.4.

Return to the problems on Handout 7.2. Solve the *join–change unknown, separate–result unknown, part-part-whole–part unknown, join–start unknown, separate–start unknown* using a strategy like the ones from Activity 8.2. Reflect on the process. Was this a straightforward process? Did you encounter any difficulty using a counting strategy to solve these problems?

As with direct modeling, using a counting strategy to solve *join–start unknown* and *separate–start unknown* problems is difficult to do. Try to use a counting strategy for these problems and identify why a counting strategy is not effective for these two types of problems.

Write about your experience, including any difficulties you encountered, in your journal.

To efficiently solve *join–start unknown* or *separate–start unknown* problems, students need another level of strategy. We will explore the final type of strategy in the next session.

Activity 8.5 Before the Next Session

5 minutes
Handout 7.1B Developing Word Problems
Handout 8.5 Student Connections: Word Problems III

Before the next session, continue to gather information about how your students solve addition and subtraction problems. This activity is similar to the Student Connections activity from Session 6 (Handout 6.5) but this time you will be using the problems you and your team developed and recorded on Handout 7.1B.

Remember that the purpose of this and other Student Connections activities is for you to collect some data about your students that will be shared at the next meeting. Sit with students individually as they complete the tasks and record what they say and do on Handout 8.5. Adjust numbers as necessary to find the limits of your students' calculation comfort zones. Try to be as detailed as possible in describing how they approach the task, how difficult the task is for them, what errors they make, and anything else of interest that happens during the interview. Using your students' responses, be prepared to report back next time whether you would like to change the difficulty ranking you had made for any of the problems.

Activity 8.6 Lesson Design Notes

5 minutes

The key ideas for this session are

- Children invent their own ways of solving mathematics problems, and understanding these strategies helps teachers to develop and support effective learning experiences.
- Solving problems using counting strategies is a natural progression from direct modeling and is a more efficient step requiring a level of abstract thinking.
- *Counting on* and *counting down* are two kinds of counting strategies.

Reflect on what you learned during this session and how the ideas apply to each of the three themes in your Lesson Design Notes. A few prompts related to the themes follow. These are merely suggestions and should not limit your reflection or the ideas you capture.

- Where do you want to go?
  - In Activity 8.1, you discussed the progression that children make from using direct modeling strategies to counting strategies. How does this inform your goals for your students?

- Where are you now?
  - In Activities 8.1 and 8.2, you examined the strategy of counting. What did you learn that helps you identify where your students are in their understanding of addition and subtraction?
- What is the best way to get there?
  - How do you support students in moving from direct modeling to counting strategies?
  - In Activity 8.3, you analyzed sample addition and subtraction lessons. What ideas from the sample lessons are you interested in trying out in your classroom?

References and Resources

Carpenter, T. P., Fennema, E., Franke, M. L., Levi, L., & Empson, S. B. (1999). *Children's mathematics: Cognitively guided instruction.* Portsmouth, NH: Heinemann.

Clemson University, & Carolina Biological Supply Company. (2009). In *Developing number concepts: Like and unlike. Math out of the box: Grade K.* Burlington, NC: Carolina Biological Supply Company.

Clemson University, & Carolina Biological Supply Company. (2009). In *Developing number concepts: Families and facts. Math out of the box: Grade 1.* Burlington, NC: Carolina Biological Supply Company.

Dolk, M. & Fosnot, C. T. (2006). *Fostering children's mathematical development: The landscape of learning* [CD-ROM]. Portsmouth, NH: Heinemann.

Fosnot, C. T., & Dolk, M. (2001). *Young mathematicians at work: Constructing number sense, addition, and subtraction.* Portsmouth, NH: Heinemann.

Fuson, K. C. (2004). Pre-K to Grade 2 goals and standards: Achieving 21st century mastery for all. In D. H. Clements, J. Sarama, & A.-M. DiBiase (Eds.), *Engaging young children in mathematics: Standards for early childhood mathematics education* (pp. 105–148). Mahwah, NJ: Lawrence Erlbaum.

Kilpatrick, J., Swafford, J., & Findell, B. (Eds.). (2001). *Adding it up: Helping children learn mathematics.* Washington, DC: National Academies Press.

Lesson 18: Separating Sets

Desired Outcomes

- Students will explore separating sets.
- Students will describe the action of subtraction verbally.
- Students will describe the action of subtraction in writing.

Teacher Information

In Lesson 18, students explore sets with different quantities and describe subtraction situations as objects are removed from the sets. Students create sets using concrete materials and perform the action of "taking away" part of the whole set.

Various language patterns are used as students express their experiences and observations. The role of zero is discussed as students are presented with taking away zero objects from a set. Students work in pairs to represent subtraction facts and then share descriptions with the whole group as they develop the concept of subtraction.

Teacher Preparation

- Choose a literature selection about counting back, such as *Ten Dogs in the Window* by Claire Masurel or *Ten Silly Dogs* by Lisa Flather.
- Prepare a set of 20 counting links for each pair of students. Plastic bags are provided for managing the collections.
- Assemble for distribution: counting links and Student Record Books.
- Provide students with crayons, scissors, and glue, which are not included in the kit.

Materials

For the class

1 magnetic trifold board
6 magnetic circle counters

For each pair of students

20 counting links
1 small plastic bag

For each student

Student Record Book

Needed but not supplied

Literature selection
Crayons
Scissors
Glue

Vocabulary

Analyze: To examine the parts.

Equation: A mathematical statement that two things are equal, written with an equal sign.

Number sentence: A mathematical statement containing three parts: a left-side expression, a relation symbol, and a right-side expression.

Pattern: Elements arranged according to a rule or plan.

Relationship: A meaningful connection.

Represent: To show in another way.

Procedure for the Lesson

Engage

Exploring Solutions

1. Gather the students at an area designated for group meetings and read a literature selection about counting back, such as *Ten Dogs in the Window* by Claire Masurel or *Ten Silly Dogs* by Lisa Flather.

2. Lead a discussion about how the number of dogs becomes smaller each time one leaves. Ask,

   What do you notice happening in the story?

   What happens each time a dog is taken away in the story?

Investigate

Creating Sets

1. Arrange students to sit with a partner. Present the following story to the students: *There were six frogs on the bank of the pond. Two jumped in the water. How many were left on the bank?* Explain that students will act out the parts of the story. Ask,

   How many students are needed to tell the story?

   What happens in the story?

   What action needs to happen? How do you know?

2. Choose six students to come to the front of the group. Have two of the students jump into an imaginary pond. Have each pair discuss the action and a way to describe it. Ask,

   What description did you hear from your partner?

   How many frogs were in the whole set?

   How many frogs jumped into the pond?

   How many frogs are left on the bank?

3. As students share, display the trifold board and record their descriptions on the board. Ask,

   How would you represent the story in a drawing?

   How can you count to find the solution to the story problem?

4. Create a drawing on the board to represent the story and action of subtraction. Explain that counting back is one way to find out how many are left after some are taken away. Choose a student to count back from six to represent the number of frogs that jumped into the pond.

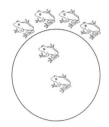

There were 6 frogs.
2 jumped in the pond.
4 frogs are on the bank.

If you take away 2 from 6, you get 4.

There are 6, and 2 leave. Now there are 4.

5. Have the two students return to the group of six. Present the story to the students again, this time with the number of frogs that jump into the pond changed to zero. *There were six frogs on the bank of the pond. None of the frogs jumped in the water. How many were left on the bank?* Ask,

How did the number of frogs change?

6. Have students again discuss with their partner the action in the story and a way to describe it. Ask,

What happens when no frogs are removed from the group?

How can you describe the action?

How many frogs were in the whole set?

How many frogs jumped into the pond?

How many frogs remain on the bank?

7. Explain that when zero is taken away the set stays the same because nothing is removed. Record the students' descriptions on the board. Ask,

How can this story be represented on the board with counters?

8. Place six magnetic circle counters on the board around the edge of a circle drawn with the black marker w/eraser.

9. Distribute the Student Record Books and have the students locate the Reflective Practice for Lesson 18. Lead the students as they read the story from the Reflective Practice.

10. Distribute a set of counting links to each pair of students. Explain that each pair will use the links to solve the story problem. Direct each student to represent the story using a drawing and words. Students will need access to crayons. Ask,

Does anyone have any questions about the story problem?

There were 6 frogs.
2 jumped in the pond.
4 frogs are on the bank.

If you take away 2 from 6, you get 4.
There are 6, and 2 leave. Now there are 4.

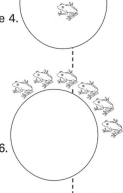

There were 6 frogs.
None of them jumped in the pond.
There are 6 frogs on the bank.

There are 6, and 0 leave. Now there are 6.
If you take away 0 from 6, you have 6.

Reflect

Sharing Solutions

1. After the students have represented the story problem, have them bring their Reflective Practice sheet to share with the group. Choose several students to describe their solution. Ask,

   How did you solve the problem?

   How did you represent the problem with a drawing? Words?

   Did anyone represent the problem a different way? Explain.

2. Encourage students to make positive comments and ask questions as others share.

Apply

Making Connections

The following activities can be used with whole groups, small groups, or individuals, depending on the needs of your students. The activities connect to past and future learning.

Story Problems

Provide other story problems for students to represent using drawings and words. Make available counting links, drawing paper, and crayons available for students to use to find solutions to the problems. Give students an opportunity to share their representations with the class or others in the school. Use story problems such as the following:

Eight squirrels were climbing a tree. Five jumped to the ground. How many squirrels were left in the tree?

Five books were on the table. A student picked up two. How many books were still on the table?

Seven birds landed on the branch. Four flew away. How many were still on the branch?

Counting Back

Provide students with counting links and have them connect nine links. Direct the students to remove one link and count back to eight. Repeat removing and counting back until two links remain. Have the students then switch and add the counters back on, counting up each time. Have students continue counting on and counting back beginning with other quantities.

Creating Problems

Provide pairs of students with a Domino Card Set. Have each pair divide the set so that one student has cards 1–4 and the other student has cards 5–9. Direct the students to mix up their individual sets and then have the students with the higher numbers in each pair draw a card from the pile and place it in front of them. Have the other student in each pair draw a card from their pile and place it to the right of the first number. Have the students write a number sentence in words describing the action and represent the number sentence with a drawing. Students will need access to drawing paper and crayons.

Connected Practice

Assign the Connected Practice for Lesson 18 from the Student Record Book. Explain that students will cut out the numbers at the bottom of the sheet and glue them in the appropriate box to show the solution to each subtraction problem. Students will need access to scissors and glue.

Teacher Reflection

What did I learn about my students as they described problem solutions?

What did my students learn as they represented subtraction story problems?

Assessment

- Are students able to explore separating sets?
- Are students able to describe the action of subtraction verbally?
- Are students able to describe the action of subtraction in writing?

Information can be gathered from

Class Discussion

Teacher Observation

Individual and Group Questioning

Exploring Solutions

Creating Sets

Sharing Solutions

Student Record Book

Making Connections

Lesson 18: Separating Sets
Reflective Practice

Name: _____ **Date:** _____

There were five balls on the table. Three rolled off. How many balls are left on the table?

Represent the problem in a drawing and words.

Representations will vary.

Lesson 18: Separating Sets
Connected Practice: Developing Number Concepts

Name: _____   Date: _____

Cut out the numbers below and glue them in the box to show the solution to the subtraction action.

Objects	Answer
🔒🔒🔒 🔒̸🔒̸🔒̸	3
💡 💡̸💡̸💡̸💡̸💡̸💡̸	1
🌲🌲🌲🌲 🌲̸	4
⭐⭐⭐⭐⭐ ⭐̸⭐̸⭐̸	5

| 3 | 5 | 4 | 1 |

Source: Clemson University, & Carolina Biological Supply Company. (2009). *Developing number concepts: Like and unlike* (Math Out of the Box: Grade K). Burlington, NC: Carolina Biological Supply Company. Reprinted with permission.

Lesson 8: Describing Addition Patterns

Desired Outcomes

- Students will analyze addition patterns using a number line.
- Students will describe patterns in basic facts that add zero, one, or two.
- Students will compare strategies for developing fluency with addition facts.

Teacher Information

The ability to quickly recall correct answers to basic number facts is a necessary part of being successful in other aspects of mathematics. Written and mental computation, elements of problem solving, and computational estimation all require these basic skills. Developing a strong foundation in this area will help students move from counting to quick recall of the facts needed for real-world mathematics.

Students begin by analyzing addition facts and looking for patterns. In Lesson 8, students explore the addition facts that add zero, one, and two by using a number line to count on to find the sums. Students summarize their findings on a chart and then individually solve problems that add zero, one, or two.

Teacher Preparation

- On a sheet of newsprint, prepare a chart with the title "Adding 0, 1, or 2."
- Identify an area of the classroom or hallway to display the Floor Number Card Set from zero to ten.
- Assemble for distribution: Student Record Books and Bright Idea Pencils.

Materials

For the class

1 sheet of newsprint
Floor Number Card Set
1 black marker w/eraser
Bright Idea Marker

For each student

Student Record Book
Bright Idea Pencil

Vocabulary

Analyze: To examine the parts.

Equation: A mathematical statement that two things are equal, written with an equal sign.

Number sentence: A mathematical statement containing three parts: a left-side expression, a relation symbol, and a right-side expression.

Pattern: Elements arranged according to a rule or plan.

Relationship: A meaningful connection.

Represent: To show in another way.

Procedure for the Lesson

Engage

Exploring the Number Line

1. Choose a large area of the classroom or hallway to display the Floor Number Card Set. Display the cards zero to ten on the floor, spacing each card about a foot apart. Ask,

   What do you notice about the class number line?

   What do you know about the number zero?

2. Choose a student to come to the front of the room and stand at the number four. Direct the student to move zero spaces. Ask,

   What number on the number line is the student standing at now? Why?

   What happens to a number when you add it to zero?

3. Display the chart entitled, "Adding 0, 1, or 2." As students share, summarize their ideas on the chart.

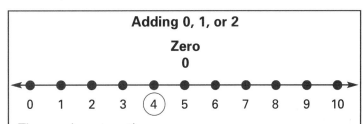

Adding 0, 1, or 2

Zero

0

The number stays the same.

You don't move on the number line.

When a zero is added to any number, the answer is still that number, like 4 + 0 = 4 or 10 + 0 = 10.

Investigate

Counting On

1. Explain that with facts that add zero it is not necessary to move to another number on the number line. Ask,

   What happens when one is added to a number?

2. Write the following story on the chart: *Five goats were in the barn eating. One more goat comes into the barn. How many goats are in the barn?* Ask,

   What is the question in this problem?

   How can the solution be found using the number line?

3. Have a different student stand at the number five and then move to the number six on the number line. Represent the number line on the chart and show the action of adding one more to the number five. Ask,

What is the answer when one more is added to five?

What would be the answer if one more is added to six? Seven? Eight? Nine?

4. Have the student move to the number seven on the number line and continue to move to the appropriate number as students add one more each time. Ask,

What do you know about adding one more to any number?

5. As students share, summarize their ideas on the chart and record the addition equations that add one with sums through 20.

Five goats were in the barn eating. One more goat comes into the barn. How many goats are in the barn?

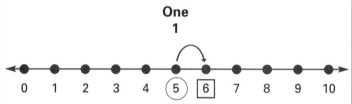

Each time one is added you count on one more to the next counting number.

One added to any number is the next number on the number line.

1 + 1 = 2	7 + 1 = 8	13 + 1 = 14
2 + 1 = 3	8 + 1 = 9	14 + 1 = 15
3 + 1 = 4	9 + 1 = 10	15 + 1 = 16
4 + 1 = 5	10 + 1 = 11	16 + 1 = 17
5 + 1 = 6	11 + 1 = 12	17 + 1 = 18
6 + 1 = 7	12 + 1 = 13	18 + 1 = 19
		19 + 1 = 20

---

6. Add the following story to the chart: *Three cows were grazing in the field. Two more cows joined them. How many cows are grazing in the field?* Ask,

What is happening in the story?

What is the question being asked?

How can the solution be found using the number line?

7. Select a different student to stand at the number three and count two spaces to the number five. Draw a number line showing the action of adding two more to the number three on the chart. Ask,

What is the answer when two more is added to three?

What would be the answer if two more is added to five? Seven?

8. Have the student move to the number seven on the number line and continue to move to the appropriate number as students add two more each time. Ask,

What do you know about adding two more to any number?

9. As students share, summarize their ideas on the chart and record the addition equations that add two with sums through 20.

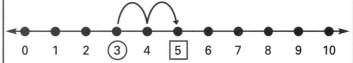

Three cows were grazing in the field. Two more cows joined them. How many cows are grazing in the field?

When you add two to a number, you count on two times; like with the number 3, you count 4, 5.

The answer is more than the first number or the second number being added.

If you add two to a number, skip the next counting number, and the answer is the following counting number. If you begin on 3, you skip 4, and 5 is the answer.

1 + 2 = 3	7 + 2 = 9	13 + 2 = 15
2 + 2 = 4	8 + 2 = 10	14 + 2 = 16
3 + 2 = 5	9 + 2 = 11	15 + 2 = 17
4 + 2 = 6	10 + 2 = 12	16 + 2 = 18
5 + 2 = 7	11 + 2 = 13	17 + 2 = 19
6 + 2 = 8	12 + 2 = 14	18 + 2 = 20

10. Distribute the Student Record Books and have the students locate the Reflective Practice for Lesson 8. Direct the students to use the number lines to solve each of the story problems and write an equation for each problem.

Reflect

Sharing Mathematical Thinking

1. After the students have finished solving the story problems, lead a discussion about adding zero, one, or two more. Ask,

   What do you know about adding zero to a number? Adding one to a number?

   Adding two to a number?

2. Write an equation on the chart using different formats, such as $7 + 1 = 8$, $\begin{array}{r} 7 \\ +\,1 \\ \hline 8 \end{array}$, $7 + 1 = 1 + 7$, and $8 = 7 + 1$. Lead a discussion about the different ways to write equations, horizontally with the sum on either side of the equal symbol, or vertically. Ask,

   How are these equations alike? Different?

   What is true of any equation?

   Are there any new ideas that can be added to the class chart?

3. Add any new ideas to the class chart using the Bright Idea Marker.

Apply

Making Connections

The following activities can be used with whole groups, small groups, or individuals, depending on the needs of your students. The activities connect to past and future learning.

Adding With Ten Frames

Provide two-colored counters, ten frames, and drawing paper for students. Encourage them to display two ten frames and use the counters to combine sets to create facts that add one more. Have students work in pairs or small groups to represent all the facts they can create that add one.

Count On

Provide connecting counters, drawing paper, and crayons for students. Have them create facts with the connecting counters that add one or two more, such as $9 + 1$ or $5 + 2$. The students then write the facts on the drawing paper.

Connected Practice

Assign the Connected Practice for Lesson 8 from the Student Record Book. Explain that students will solve and represent basic facts that add zero, one, and two. Have the students change any

Assessment

- Are students able to analyze addition patterns using a number line?
- Are students able to describe patterns in basic facts that add zero, one, or two?
- Are students able to compare strategies for developing fluency with addition facts?

Information can be gathered from

Class Discussion

Teacher Observation

Individual and Group Questioning

Exploring the Number Line

Counting On

Sharing Mathematical Thinking

Student Record Book

Making Connections

Lesson 8: Describing Addition Patterns
Reflective Practice

Name: _____ **Date:** _____

1. Use the number line to solve the story problem.

   Mr. Lewis had 13 pigs. He bought 1 pig at the market. How many pigs does Mr. Lewis have now?

   14

   Write the equation for the story problem.

   13 + 1 = 14

2. Use the number line to solve the story problem.

   Twelve geese landed on the pond. Two more geese joined them. How many geese are on the pond?

   14

   Write the equation for the story problem.

   12 + 2 = 14

3. **Solve the problems.**

Set A.

11 + 1 = __12__   1 + 14 = __15__   9 + 2 = __11__

4 + 2 = __6__   12 + 0 = __12__   2 + 7 = __9__

$$
\begin{array}{r} 15 \\ + 1 \\ \hline 16 \end{array} \qquad
\begin{array}{r} 8 \\ + 2 \\ \hline 10 \end{array} \qquad
\begin{array}{r} 10 \\ + 1 \\ \hline 11 \end{array} \qquad
\begin{array}{r} 6 \\ + 0 \\ \hline 6 \end{array}
$$

Set B.

1 + 5 = __6__   13 + 2 = __15__   5 + 2 = __7__

0 + 2 = __2__   17 + 1 = __18__   11 + 2 = __13__

$$
\begin{array}{r} 16 \\ + 2 \\ \hline 18 \end{array} \qquad
\begin{array}{r} 7 \\ + 0 \\ \hline 7 \end{array} \qquad
\begin{array}{r} 18 \\ + 1 \\ \hline 19 \end{array} \qquad
\begin{array}{r} 12 \\ + 2 \\ \hline 14 \end{array}
$$

Lesson 8: Describing Addition Patterns
Connected Practice: Developing Number Concepts

Name: _____   **Date:** _____

0   1   2   3   4   5   6   7   8   9   10

1. Solve the addition facts by adding 0, 1, and 2.

$4 + 0 =$ __4__ $5 + 1 =$ __6__ $8 + 2 =$ __10__

$6 + 2 =$ __8__ $7 + 1 =$ __8__ $6 + 0 =$ __6__

2. Solve the problems.

$11 + 1 =$ __12__   __14__ $= 13 + 1$ $18 + 1 =$ __19__

$13 + 0 = 0 +$ __13__ $12 + 1 =$ __13__ $2 + 15 =$ __17__

$$\begin{array}{r} 17 \\ +\ 0 \\ \hline 17 \end{array} \qquad \begin{array}{r} 1 \\ +\ 9 \\ \hline 10 \end{array} \qquad \begin{array}{r} 6 \\ +\ 2 \\ \hline 8 \end{array} \qquad \begin{array}{r} 14 \\ +\ 2 \\ \hline 16 \end{array}$$

 Source: Clemson University, & Carolina Biological Supply Company. (2009). *Developing number concepts: Families and facts* (Math Out of the Box: Grade 1). Burlington, NC: Carolina Biological Supply Company. Reprinted with permission.

Handout 8.3C

Investigating Instructional Materials: Kindergarten Lesson

Examine the lesson on Handout 8.3A and answer the questions below.

Lesson: *Math Out of the Box: Kindergarten, Teacher's Guide Module A* (pp. 159–166)

What big ideas, strategies, and mathematical models are being developed in this lesson?
What are the important mathematical concepts underlying the lesson? How does the lesson reflect the concepts from the Common Core State Standards? What skills and knowledge are required to complete the tasks?
Which strands of mathematical proficiency are represented in this lesson?

The lesson suggests reading a book about counting back, acting out the problem with students, and creating a drawing on the board to represent the story and action of subtraction. How does each of these help students build strategies for solving word problems?

The lesson suggests that pairs of students solve the story problem. What opportunities for learning are provided for students who work together? What are some of the challenges that you have had with pairs of students working together?

The lesson suggests that students connect nine links and then count back as they remove one link at a time. How does this support students in using a counting strategy?

What are the strengths of this lesson?	What are some limitations, questions, and concerns that you have about the lesson?

Handout 8.3D

Investigating Instructional Materials: First Grade Lesson

Examine the lesson on Handout 8.3B and answer the questions below.

Lesson: *Math Out of the Box: Grade One, Teacher's Guide Module A* (pp. 77–85)

What big ideas, strategies, and mathematical models are being developed in this lesson?
What are the important mathematical concepts underlying the lesson? How does the lesson reflect the concepts from the Common Core State Standards? What skills and knowledge are required for students to complete the tasks?
Which strands of mathematical proficiency are represented in this lesson?

How does this lesson support students' use of counting strategies? How does the use of the number line encourage students' use of counting strategies? How might the use of counters or cubes, instead of the number line, influence the strategies used by students?

How does the selection of adding 0, 1, or 2 encourage the use of counting strategies?

How might the lesson and the use of the number line be adapted for other problem types?

What are the strengths of this lesson?	What are some limitations, questions, and concerns that you have about the lesson?

Handout 8.3E
Investigating Your Instructional Materials

Examine a lesson from your instructional materials that focuses on models for addition and/or subtraction concepts and answer the questions below. You will use your responses to develop the lesson in Session 12.

Lesson: _____   Pages: _____

What big ideas, strategies, and mathematical models are being developed in this lesson?

What are the important mathematical concepts underlying the lesson? How does the lesson reflect the concepts from the Common Core State Standards? What skills and knowledge are required for students to complete the tasks?

What are the similarities and differences between this lesson and the sample lesson from Handout 8.3A or 8.3B?

Which strands of mathematical proficiency are represented in this lesson?

What are the strengths of this lesson?	What are some limitations, questions, and concerns that you have about the lesson? What misunderstandings and difficulties might your students encounter?

Handout 8.4
Counting Strategies

Counting		
Counting on from first	• Saying the first addend • Counting forward from the first addend • Stopping when the number of counting steps in the second addend have been completed	• Join–result unknown • Part-part-whole–whole unknown • Compare–compared set unknown
Counting on from larger	• Mirroring previous strategy, except beginning counting with the larger of the two addends	• Join–result unknown • Part-part-whole–whole unknown • Compare–compared set unknown
Counting on to	• Counting sequence begins with smaller given number • Ending sequence with larger given number • Keeping track of the number of counting words gives the answer	• Join–change unknown
Counting down	• Beginning counting sequence with the larger number given in the problem • Counting backwards until the number of counting steps in the smaller number have been completed	• Separate–result unknown • Compare–difference unknown
Counting down to	• Beginning counting sequence with the larger number given in the problem • Ending backward counting sequence when the smaller number is reached • Keeping track of the number of counting words in the sequence gives the solution	• Separate–change unknown • Part-part-whole–part unknown • Compare–difference unknown
Trial and error	• Trying out a number for the start of the problem • Joining or separating the change quantity in the problem • Asking, "Did the quantity I try at the start of the problem get me to the result?" If not, trying a different number for the start of the problem.	• Join–start unknown • Separate–start unknown

Handout 8.5
Student Connections: Word Problems III

Record the problems you developed in the appropriate cells, and adjust the numbers in the problems to appropriately meet the needs of each student you are interviewing. The purpose of this activity is to collect information on the mathematical limit for each student. Provide counters, blank paper, and pencils for students. Allow them to use any method to solve these problems. Write notes here about the strategies students use to solve these problems.

Problem A			
Problem type		Difficulty	
Student 1			
Student 2			
Student 3			

Problem B			
Problem type		Difficulty	
Student 1			
Student 2			
Student 3			
Problem C			
Problem type		Difficulty	
Student 1			
Student 2			
Student 3			

Session 9

Children's Strategies: Numerical Reasoning

Overview

What strategies do students develop next in the learning progression for solving addition and subtraction problems?

Description

As we have discussed in previous sessions, the progression that most students follow as they develop increasingly sophisticated strategies is one of the best-understood aspects of mathematics learning. Students move from counting strategies to more abstract thinking that involves numerical reasoning and recalled and derived number facts for solving addition and subtraction problems.

Key Ideas

- Children invent their own ways of solving mathematics problems, and understanding these strategies helps teachers to develop and support effective learning experiences.
- Solving problems using numerical reasoning is a natural progression from counting and is a more efficient strategy that is based on abstract thinking.
- Known facts, derived facts, and flexibility with number combinations are numerical reasoning strategies that young children develop.

Outline of Activities

- 9.1 The Progression of Children's Strategies (20 minutes)
- 9.2 Examining Numerical Reasoning (20 minutes)
- 9.3 Recognizing Strategies (20 minutes)
- 9.4 The Teacher's Role in the Development of Children's Strategies (20 minutes)
- 9.5 Before the Next Session (5 minutes)
- 9.6 Lesson Design Notes (5 minutes)

What to Bring

- Notes and student work: Student Connections activities (Handouts 5.5, 6.5, and 8.5)

To Complete Before Session 10

- Investigating Instructional Materials activity with NCTM Illuminations

Facilitator Notes   Session 9

Children's Strategies: Numerical Reasoning

If this is your first time facilitating the group, please refer to the more detailed facilitator guidelines in the Introduction. As the facilitator, it is generally your job to keep the conversation flowing and watch the clock. Use your judgment to decide when it's appropriate to extend a session for good conversation or when it's time to move on to the next activity. Remember to keep the group norms posted and revise them, as a group, as necessary.

Before the Session

- Make copies of the following handouts for each team member:
    - ☐ 9.3 Identify the Strategy
- Gather the following materials to be used in this session:
    - ☐ Group norms (from Activity 1.4)
- Remind team members to bring the following items from previous sessions:
    - ☐ Journal (and writing instruments)
    - ☐ Completed homework, Handouts 5.5, 6.5, 8.5 Student Connections: Word Problems I, II, and III

During the Session

- Post group norms, and revise as a group as necessary.
- Activity 9.5: facilitate pairing, if necessary.

After the Session

- Remind team members of homework, Investigating Instructional Materials activity with NCTM Illuminations.
- Pass any team materials to the next facilitator.

Activity 9.1 The Progression of Children's Strategies

20 minutes

Read the following descriptions of solution strategies.

Problem: There were 16 children on the playground, and some of them went back to the classroom. Now there are 7 children on the playground. How many children went back to the classroom?

- Ingrid counts out 16 blocks. Next she pushes a few blocks aside and counts the ones still in the pile and finds she has 11 in the pile. She pushes a few more out of the pile and counts again. This time she has 8 in the pile. She pushes 1 more out of the pile and counts. Now she has 7 in the pile. Finally she counts the pushed-aside blocks, saying "1, 2, 3, 4, 5, 6, 7, 8, 9—so 9 children went back."
- Dino says 16, then pauses. Next he counts back, saying "15, 14, 13, 12, 11, 10, 9, 8, 7," putting a finger up for each count and stopping at 7. He then counts the number of fingers extended, saying "1, 2, 3, 4, 5, 6, 7, 8, 9," touching each finger to his chin as he counts. He says, "There were 9 children who went back."
- Scott says, "I know 16 minus 8 equals 8, because that's a double, and 16 minus something is 7. Oh, I know, 16 minus 9 is 7 because if you take away one more, you end up with one less. There were 9 children who went back."
- Patricia says, "If 6 children went back, there would be 10 children left, but that's too many left. That means three more must have gone in so that the number left would be 7. That means that 6 plus 3 . . . (pauses) so 9 children went back."

Discuss the following questions with your group:

- What type of problem is this playground problem?
- What strategy did Ingrid use? How do you know?
- What strategy did Dino use? How do you know?
- Describe Scott's and Patricia's strategies. How do their strategies differ from Ingrid's and Dino's?

Considerable research from all over the world shows that children move through a fairly predictable progression composed of three types of strategies for finding the sums of single-digit numbers (Kirkpatrick, Swafford, & Findell, 2001). In Session 7, you examined the strategy of *direct modeling,* the most basic and universally accessible strategy for students. Ingrid uses this strategy in the playground problem.

Over time, direct modeling gives way to a more efficient strategy, counting. In Session 8, you examined some of the ways *counting strategies* can be used to solve various types of problems. Counting strategies naturally emerge from student experiences with direct modeling because they are closely related to direct modeling but require the student to abstract one of the quantities in the problem. Dino uses this strategy in the playground problem.

The final strategy, which Scott and Patricia use in the playground problem vignettes, is really a collection of strategies that involve reasoning about numbers themselves without having to represent those quantities with objects or pictures. We will refer to these types of strategies as *numerical reasoning.*

While this progression of strategies is well-documented, children do not move in a linear trajectory through the strategies, adopting first one and then the next in sequence. They usually use several strategies at the same time for extended periods, and often use different strategies for different numbers or different problem situations (Fuson, 2004). It is important for students to maintain the ability to use all of these strategies so that they can choose an appropriate strategy when faced with an unfamiliar or more challenging problem.

Discuss the following questions with your group:

- Think about your own students. Can you think of children who use each of these types of strategies? For which of your students is direct modeling the predominant strategy? For which of your students is counting the predominant strategy? For which of your students is numerical reasoning the predominant strategy? Which of your students have flexibility with all of these strategies?

- What do you think you can do to help your students develop flexibility in using all of these strategies?

Activity 9.2 Examining Numerical Reasoning

20 minutes

Handout 2.3 Components of a Learning Landscape

Handout 5.5 Student Connections: Word Problems I

Handout 6.5 Student Connections: Word Problems II

Handout 8.5 Student Connections: Word Problems III

Scott's and Patricia's strategies in the vignettes in Activity 9.1 are two examples of numerical reasoning. Scott used his knowledge of a known number combination ($16 - 8 = 8$) to break apart and determine the result for a related combination ($16 - ? = 7$). Patricia used the fact that $16 - 6 = 10$ to logically determine that $16 - 9 = 7$. As children's experiences with numbers increase, they will begin to learn number facts and apply this knowledge to solving problems. Children may learn certain number combinations before others and use these facts to derive other number combinations.

Read the following vignettes.

Problem: Yuri picked 7 pumpkins. His brother picked 6 pumpkins. How many pumpkins do the boys have together?

Vignette: Steven thinks for a moment and then says that it is 13. When asked how he knew this, Steven says, "Because 7 and 7 is 14. This is 7 and 6, so it must be one less . . . 13."

Problem: Tom had 14 books. He gave some of them away. Now Tom has 9 books. How many books did he give away?

Vignette: Victor says, "If I count back 4 from 14, I get 10. Then from 10 to 9 is 1, and 4 plus 1 is 5."

Problem: There were some apples in the cafeteria. My teacher took 4 of them. Now there are 5 apples. How many apples were in the cafeteria to start?

Vignette: Penny writes the number sentence: _ – 4 = 5. She says, "I know . . . 8 take away 4 is 4, so 9 take away 4 is 5."

Problem: Mike had 9 pennies. His mom gave him 5 more pennies. How many pennies does Mike have now?"

Vignette: Chloe does not use the manipulatives available to her. She rolls her eyes as if looking up and says, "First I can take 1 of the pennies from his mom and add it to the 9 to get 10. There are 4 pennies left in his mom's pile and 10 plus 4 is 14."

Discuss the following questions:

- What is the problem type for each of these problems?
- Each student used a kind of numerical reasoning. Describe the reasoning process each student used. What number relationship did each child use?
- Penny translated the word problem into a number sentence. How did this help her to use numerical reasoning?
- Return to your description of student strategies from previous observations (Activities 5.5, 6.5, and 8.5). Did any of your students use numerical reasoning? Share these examples with the group.
- Review the components of a learning landscape on Handout 2.3. What strategies have you listed so far? Are there strategies that you would like to add to the web based on today's session?

Activity 9.3 Recognizing Strategies

20 minutes   Handout 9.3 Identify the Strategy

Read the series of vignettes illustrating children solving addition and subtraction problems on Handout 9.3.

Discuss the following questions:

- What is the problem type for each question?
- What strategy did the student use in each vignette?

"Knowledge of developmental progressions—levels of understanding and skill, each more sophisticated than the last—is essential for high-quality teaching based on understanding both mathematics and children's thinking and learning" (Sarama & Clements, 2009, p. 17).

- What is your reaction to the preceding quotation?
- Why is it important for teachers to know problem types and strategies that students might use to solve them?
- How can this information help teachers to facilitate student learning?

Activity 9.4 The Teacher's Role in the Development of Children's Strategies

20 minutes

At several points in these sessions, you have read that children naturally develop more efficient and more abstract strategies for solving addition and subtraction problems, and that this progression can happen without instruction or guidance from adults in how and when to use the strategies. This is not to say that the teacher and the instructional choices do not matter. Well-crafted lessons, careful discussions about solution methods, and opportunities to use models all support students' development of increasingly efficient solution methods.

Researchers tell us that children begin to solve problems using direct modeling, the most basic and universally accessible strategy for students. Eventually children begin to use a more efficient strategy, counting, which relies on the ability to keep track of some quantities without physically building or drawing them. Finally, students develop the ability to reason about numbers themselves using number combinations they know to find combinations they don't know.

It is the notion that this progression of strategies happens *without instruction or guidance from adults* that can be somewhat troubling for teachers.

Read the following exchange between three kindergarten and first grade teachers, Mr. Blake, Ms. Stanton, and Ms. Zimmerman.

Mr. Blake:	My students just don't seem to be developing more efficient strategies for solving addition and subtraction word problems. Virtually all of them are still using direct modeling, and none of them seem to be moving toward counting strategies or numerical reasoning . . . not by a long shot. They are really good at building or drawing solutions, and I really encourage that, but I worry that maybe they are too comfortable with direct modeling. Should I push them to try other strategies? Should I take the blocks away?
Ms. Stanton:	I know just what you mean. My students were in the same boat, so I started showing them how to solve problems in more "grown up" ways. Now I have my students copy what I do on the board so they will see how to use more efficient strategies. I mean, if they don't start learning these processes, they'll never survive in second grade. I've started telling them that I don't want to see any more blocks or pictures. That's too babyish for them. A few of them have started to come around, but a lot of them just use their fingers under the table where they think I can't see them. I'm at a loss, too.
Ms. Zimmerman:	I always wonder about what my role is in helping children develop efficient strategies. I find myself vacillating between being completely hands off and just letting the learning happen, and being really directive and guiding them to think in a particular way. I finally came to the conclusion that neither one of those really works. There must be a role for the teacher that is somewhere in between, but I'm not sure what it is. What can I do as the teacher that encourages students to develop thinking strategies without imposing my adult thinking on them?

Discuss the following questions with your group:

- If you were the fourth teacher in this exchange, what would you say to your colleagues? Which of them expressed a feeling you have had?
- How would you respond to Ms. Zimmerman's question, "What can I do as the teacher that encourages students to develop thinking strategies without imposing my adult thinking on them?"
- What role do you think classroom interactions play in the development of student strategies? What is the role of student-student conversations? What is the role of teacher-student conversations?

Activity 9.5 Before the Next Session

5 minutes

Before the next session, visit NCTM's Illuminations website (http://illuminations.nctm.org/) and identify an activity or lesson to try in your classroom. According to NCTM, the site is designed to

- Provide standards-based resources that improve the teaching and learning of mathematics for all students.
- Provide materials that illuminate the vision for school mathematics set forth in *Principles and Standards for School Mathematics.*

The Illuminations site includes four sections: activities, lessons, standards, and web links. For this activity, use the activities or lessons sections for your search. Try to find a lesson that is related to addition or subtraction in kindergarten or first grade. You may want to work in pairs to plan and implement the activity or lesson.

Before you use the lesson, write in your journal about your goals and expectations. Consider the following questions:

- Why did you choose this lesson or activity?
- What is the goal or learning objective for the lesson or activity?
- How is the lesson or activity connected to the components of a learning landscape, the Common Core State Standards, or the five strands of mathematical proficiency?
- How do you think students will respond to the tasks?
- What modifications will you make?

After you teach the lesson or use the activity, collect student work or other artifacts. Take some time to reflect on what happened. Write responses to the following questions in your journal:

- What aspects of the activity or lesson were successful?
- What aspects of the lessons went according to your expectations? Were there any unexpected reactions from students?
- What evidence do you have that students met the goal?
- What was challenging about using the lesson?
- What would you do differently? How would you advise other teachers who want to use the lesson?

You will share the results in Session 10. You will also be using the results of this activity to design the prototype lesson. Save your materials, student work, and reflections for Session 12.

Activity 9.6 Lesson Design Notes

5 minutes

The key ideas for this session are

- Children invent their own ways of solving mathematics problems, and understanding these strategies helps teachers to develop and support effective learning experiences.
- Solving problems using numerical reasoning is a natural progression from counting and is a more efficient strategy based on abstract thinking.
- Known facts, derived facts, and flexibility with number combinations are numerical reasoning strategies that young children develop.

Reflect on what you learned during this session and how the ideas apply to each of the three themes in your Lesson Design Notes. A few prompts related to the themes follow. These are merely suggestions and should not limit your reflection or the ideas you capture.

- Where do you want to go?
  o In Activities 9.1 and 9.2, you explored numerical reasoning strategies. How does this inform your goals for students?

- Where are you now?
  o In Activity 9.1, you examined the progression of strategies. What did you learn that helps you identify where your students are in their understanding of addition and subtraction?

- What is the best way to get there?
  o In Activity 9.4, you listened to an exchange among several teachers. What are some ideas that came up about how to support students to move from direct modeling to counting to numerical reasoning strategies?

References and Resources

Carpenter, T. P., Fennema, E., Franke, M. L., Levi, L., & Empson, S. B. (1999). *Children's mathematics: Cognitively guided instruction.* Portsmouth, NH: Heinemann.

Fosnot, C. T., & Dolk, M. (2001). *Young mathematicians at work: Constructing number sense, addition, and subtraction.* Portsmouth, NH: Heinemann.

Fuson, K. C. (2004). Pre-K to Grade 2 goals and standards: Achieving 21st century mastery for all. In D. H. Clements, J. Sarama, & A.-M. DiBiase (Eds.), *Engaging young children in mathematics: Standards for early childhood mathematics education* (pp. 105–148). Mahwah, NJ: Lawrence Erlbaum.

Kilpatrick, J., Swafford, J., & Findell, B. (Eds.). (2001). *Adding it up: Helping children learn mathematics.* Washington, DC: National Academies Press.

Sarama, J., & Clements, D. H. (2009). *Early childhood mathematics education research: Learning trajectories for young children.* New York: Routledge.

Handout 9.3
Identify the Strategy

1	*Sally had 8 bracelets. She bought 5 more bracelets. How many bracelets does Sally have now?*	Problem Type
	Sharon: It's 13. Teacher: Okay, how did you get 13? Sharon: Because 8 plus 2 is 10. But then 2 plus 3 is 5 and she wanted to buy 5 more bracelets. So you take care of 2 and then you would need to add 3 more. So add 3 more and you get 13.	Strategy
2	*Donna has 7 toy cars. She wants to have 11 toy cars. How many more does she need to buy?*	Problem Type
	Wallace grabs a handful of blocks. He counts out a group of 7 blocks and sets it aside, counting with each block: "8, 9, 10, 11." He selects additional blocks one by one into a second group. When he reaches 11, he counts the number of blocks in the second group . . . "4."	Strategy
3	*Alex drew 11 pictures. He gave 5 pictures to his friends. How many pictures does Alex have left?*	Problem Type
	Abbey makes 11 marks on the paper. She crosses out 5 of the marks. She counts the marks that are not crossed out . . . "6."	Strategy
4	*Yesterday Trevor sold 5 candy bars. Today he sold 9 more candy bars. How many candy bars has he sold altogether?*	Problem Type
	Janet: [Counts on her fingers] He sold 14. Teacher: How did you get 14? Janet: [Showing with her fingers] You go 9 . . . 10, 11, 12, 13, 14. Teacher: Why did you start with the 9? Janet: Because the 9 is the higher number and you can just add the 5.	Strategy

5	*Anna has 12 markers. Jay has 7 markers. How many more markers does Anna have?*	Problem Type
	Nick grabs some blocks from a pile. He counts out a group of 12. Then he counts out another group of 7. He puts the group of 7 blocks in a row. Then he lines up the blocks from the group of 12 next to the group of 7 until the lines are even. He puts the remaining blocks into a line and counts them . . . "5."	Strategy
6	*Megan has 8 stickers. How many more does she need to collect to have 12 stickers altogether?*	Problem Type
	Kevin: What are they again? Teacher: [Repeats the problem] Kevin: There's 8 [to himself when the teacher says that number], and 9, 10, 11, 12 [counts on his fingers as he says each number]. She needs 4 more.	Strategy

Session 10

Children's Strategies: Numerical Reasoning Using 10

Overview

What numerical reasoning strategies help move students toward continued mathematical proficiency?

Description

Research points to specific numerical reasoning strategies that are particularly powerful and help students develop flexible and efficient computational approaches. Strategies that center on the use of 10 as a landmark, including the break-apart-to-make-ten (BAMT) strategy, are commonly used by students in Japan and other countries but are less commonly used in the United States.

Key Ideas

- Numerical reasoning strategies that focus on the use of 10 as a landmark are powerful.

- Use of the BAMT strategy helps children develop flexibility with single-digit number combinations and lays the foundation for efficient computation with multidigit numbers.

- Students with greater conceptual knowledge are more likely to use sophisticated strategies and retrieve addition and subtraction combinations accurately.

Outline of Activities

- 10.1 Investigating Instructional Materials   (20 minutes)
- 10.2 Mathematical Games   (15 minutes)
- 10.3 Numerical Reasoning Strategies Based on 10   (20 minutes)
- 10.4 Landscape of Learning   (25 minutes)
- 10.5 Before the Next Session   (5 minutes)
- 10.6 Lesson Design Notes   (5 minutes)

What to Bring

- Notes: Investigating Instructional Materials activity with NCTM Illuminations
- Handouts from previous session (Handout 4.4)
- Common Core State Standards: Standards for Mathematical Content

To Complete Before Session 11

- Student Connections: Observing Children Playing Games (Handout 10.5)

Facilitator Notes   Session 10

Children's Strategies: Numerical Reasoning Using 10

If this is your first time facilitating the group, please refer to the more detailed facilitator guidelines in the Introduction. As the facilitator, it is generally your job to keep the conversation flowing and watch the clock. Use your judgment to decide when it's appropriate to extend a session for good conversation or when it's time to move on to the next activity. Remember to keep the group norms posted and revise them, as a group, as necessary.

Before the Session

- Make copies of the following handouts for each team member:
    - ☐ 10.2 Tens Games
    - ☐ 10.4 Number Sense, Addition, and Subtraction Landscape of Learning
    - ☐ 10.5 Student Connections: Observing Children Playing Games
- Gather the following materials to be used in this session:
    - ☐ Group norms (from Activity 1.4)
    - ☐ Decks of playing cards (or ask members to each bring a deck)
- Remind team members to bring the following items from previous sessions:
    - ☐ Journal (and writing instruments)
    - ☐ Investigating Instructional Materials activity with NCTM Illuminations
    - ☐ Handout 4.4
    - ☐ Common Core State Standards: Standards for Mathematical Content

During the Session

- Post group norms, and revise as a group as necessary.
- Activity 10.1: serve as timekeeper.
- Activity 10.2: facilitate partnering, if necessary.

After the Session

- Remind team members of homework, Handout 10.5 Student Connections: Observing Children Playing Games.
- Pass any team materials to the next facilitator.

Activity 10.1 Investigating Instructional Materials

20 minutes

In this activity, you will be reporting to the group about the NCTM Illuminations lesson that you taught in your classrooms. Identify a timekeeper to make sure that everyone has an opportunity to share.

Before you begin, find out if any of the group members used the same lesson or activity. If so, it may be helpful to combine their reports.

Share how the lesson or activity went and the highlights from your reflections. Use student work to illustrate your report. Some common ideas you may want to include are

- Why you selected the lesson or activity
- The goal or learning objective
- Adaptations that you made and why you made them
- Successes and challenges
- Suggestions for other teachers

Discuss any questions that come up with the group.

Activity 10.2 Mathematics Games

15 minutes   Handout 10.2 Tens Games

As you saw in Session 4, number games can provide opportunities for students to build their understanding of number and operations. They can be a motivating and engaging way for students to practice skills. Games also help students become more independent—the players decide when an answer is correct, rather than relying on the teacher to validate it.

Read the descriptions of the three games on Handout 10.2 Tens Games. Each of these games engages students in a context for finding and using combinations of 10.

Play each game with a partner.

Discuss each game with your partner using the following questions:

- How does this game support understanding of combinations of 10?
- What variations could you make that would make the game more or less challenging for some of your students?
- What questions would you ask students as they play, or after the game is finished, to find out about their mathematical learning?
- What would you look for as you observe students?

Share your partner discussion with the group.

Activity 10.3 Numerical Reasoning Strategies Based on 10

20 minutes

Reread the strategy Patricia used in Session 9 (Activity 9.1). Notice that she used numerical reasoning that used groups of 10 as the basis for thinking about the numbers.

Researchers have found that students like Patricia who use combinations of 10 to solve problems are more likely to develop mathematical proficiency than those who rely on memorization to recall number combinations. Emphasis on numerical reasoning based on 10 is a hallmark of instruction in high-performing countries such as Japan, China, and the Netherlands.

BAMT strategies can take many forms but have in common the use of decomposing and recomposing to make use of 10. The following table illustrates several examples of the use of BAMT.

Rationale/Thinking	Problems	Calculation
Decompose a teen number to 10, and then take away the rest.	14 − 5	(Think: 5 = 4 + 1) 14 − 4 = 10 10 − 1 = 9
	16 − 9	(Think: 9 = 6 + 3) 16 − 6 = 10 10 − 3 = 7
Find a convenient way to make 10, and then use the rest.	6 + 7	(Think: 7 = 4 + 3) 6 + 4 = 10 10 + 3 = 13
	8 + 5	Think: (5 = 2 + 3) 8 + 2 = 10 10 + 3 = 13
Take away 10, and then compensate by adding back the extra.	15 − 9	(Think: 9 + 1 = 10) 15 − 10 = 5 5 + 1 = 6
	14 − 8	(Think: 8 + 2 = 10) 14 − 10 = 4 4 + 2 = 6

Discuss the following:

- Identify a BAMT strategy to solve each of these number problems.

  8 + 4

  15 − 8

  5 + 7

- Did any of the students you interviewed for previous Student Connections activities use a BAMT strategy?
- Is this a strategy that is familiar to you? Is this a strategy you use?
- In your opinion, does using BAMT or another numerical reasoning strategy help or hinder students in developing fluency with single-digit number combinations (often called *basic facts*)?

Read the following quotations from Sarama and Clements (2009):

Should children memorize the basic facts? Yes . . . but this is misleading as stated. Knowledge of arithmetic *concepts* forms an organizing framework for storing arithmetic combinations. Students with greater conceptual knowledge are more likely to use sophisticated strategies and retrieve combinations accurately. That is one reason we do not prefer the term "fact"—knowing an arithmetic combination well means far more than knowing a simple, isolated "fact." (p. 132)

Ultimately, children should be able to reason strategically, adapting strategies for different situations and easily and quickly retrieve the answer to any arithmetic combination when that is appropriate. Without accurate, fluid knowledge, students are unlikely to make adequate progress in arithmetic. (p. 136)

Write in your journal:

- How could the ten frame be used to help students develop fluency with BAMT strategies?
- How can BAMT strategies support students as they begin to work with double-digit numbers? For example, how might you use a BAMT strategy to solve 28 + 7 or 64 − 5?
- What benefits can you see that could result from the use of BAMT strategies?

Activity 10.4 Landscape of Learning

25 minutes

Handout 4.4 Common Core State Standards
Handout 10.4 Number Sense, Addition, and Subtraction Landscape of Learning
Common Core State Standards: Standards for Mathematical Content

In Session 2, you started brainstorming the components of a learning landscape for number and operations in kindergarten and first grade. Recall the discussion in that session when you compared teaching and learning to planning a trip. When teachers have a "map" that described how students typically progress in their mathematical understanding, they are constantly aware of what is most important for students to learn and the many routes that students might take to get there.

In several sessions, you have added to your components of a learning landscape. We will now connect your ideas to the work of Fosnot and Dolk, who use the term *landscape of learning* to describe the progression of student thinking in mathematics. The following quotation illustrates their approach:

> The metaphor of a landscape suggests a picture of a learning terrain in which students move in meandering or direct ways as they develop strategies and ideas about mathematical topics. Along students' journeys there are moments of uncertainty, moments of potential shifts in understanding (crossroads), and moments where mathematical ideas or strategies are constructed (landmarks). Knowledge of these moments gives teachers the capacity to better understand, document, and stretch students' thinking.
>
> Maarten Dolk and Catherine Twomey Fosnot,
> *Fostering Children's Mathematical Development:*
> *The Landscape of Learning* (2006, p. vii)

Handout 10.4 is the landscape of learning for number sense, addition, and subtraction in Grades K–3. This is the model developed by Dolk and Fosnot. You will be looking more closely at the three domains of the landscape: strategies, big ideas, and mathematical models. In this activity, the landscape of learning refers to the map on Handout 10.4; the components of a learning landscape refer to the web of ideas that you have been developing on Handout 2.3 in your journal.

Because Fosnot and Dolk's landscape of learning was developed for kindergarten through third grade, it includes strategies, big ideas, and models that are further along in the landscape than those at which children typically arrive in kindergarten or first grade. However, understanding where students are heading as they move into more advanced mathematics is critical for teachers at all levels to consider.

The landscape of learning is intended to be read from bottom to top. That is, the information contained at the lower portion of the map describes basic or early strategies, big ideas, and models. As you move up the page, closer to the "horizon" depicted with a cityscape, you will see listed strategies, big ideas, and models that are more advanced or sophisticated.

Strategies

Read and highlight the strategies on Handout 10.4, which are contained within rectangles on the landscape of learning.

Discuss the following questions:

- Compare the strategies on the Dolk and Fosnot landscape with the strategies you included on your components web. What similarities and differences can you identify? Is there anything your group would like to add to your components web?

- In your experience, which strategies are typical for kindergarten? Which strategies are typical for first grade? Which strategies are more likely to emerge in the second and third grades?

Big Ideas

Read and highlight the big ideas on Handout 10.4, which are contained within the ovals on the landscape of learning.

Discuss the following questions:

- Compare the big ideas on the Dolk and Fosnot landscape with the big ideas you included on your components web. What similarities and differences can you identify? Is there anything your group would like to add to your components web?

- In your experience, which big ideas are typically addressed in kindergarten? Which big ideas are typically addressed in first grade? Which big ideas are more likely to be addressed in the second and third grades?

The landscape also contains triangles indicating mathematical models. You will review and highlight the models in the next session.

Compare the landscape of learning to the Common Core State Standards (see Handout 4.4 and Standards for Mathematical Content for your grade level).

Discuss the following questions:

- What connections do you see between the landscape of learning and the sequence of learning objectives in the Common Core State Standards?

- What are the differences?

- Are there ideas from the Common Core State Standards that you want to add to your components web?

Reflect and write in your journal:

- How could the landscape of learning help you to organize your knowledge about how your students learn mathematics?

- How can it help you to plan lessons and assess where students are in their mathematical development?

- How might it help you locate students who are on different "roads"?

- Do you recognize particular "landmarks" in student learning?

- How might the "map" help the struggling student catch up with the capable student?

- How might it continue to challenge the capable student?

Share your responses with your group members.

Activity 10.5 Before the Next Session

5 minutes   Handout 10.5 Student Connections: Observing Children Playing Games

Before the next session, select one of the games from Handout 10.2 to play with three small groups of students. Sit with each group as they play the game and record what they say and do, and record your observations on Handout 10.5. Try to be as detailed as possible in describing how they approach the games, how difficult it is for your students, what errors they make, and anything else of interest that happens during the observation.

Write in your journal about what you learned about student thinking while observing students playing these games. What approaches did the children use? Was there anything that surprised you? How will you use this information to design learning experiences for your students that encourage them to use reasoning strategies based on 10s?

Activity 10.6 Lesson Design Notes

5 minutes

The key ideas for this session are

- Numerical reasoning strategies that focus on the use of 10 as a landmark are powerful.
- Use of the BAMT strategy helps children develop flexibility with single-digit number combinations and lays the foundation for efficient computation with multidigit numbers.
- Students with greater conceptual knowledge are more likely to use sophisticated strategies and retrieve addition and subtraction combinations accurately.

Reflect on what you learned during this session and how the ideas apply to each of the three themes in your Lesson Design Notes. A few prompts related to the themes follow. These are merely suggestions and should not limit your reflection or the ideas you capture.

- Where do you want to go?
  - In Activity 10.4, you examined the landscape of learning for addition and subtraction. What are the connections between the landscape of learning and your goals for students' mathematical learning?
- Where are you now?
  - How does the landscape of learning help you understand where your students are in developing their mathematical knowledge?
  - What ideas of the landscape of learning are relevant to the notes you have captured so far?
- What is the best way to get there?
  - In Activity 10.1, you shared and discussed a mathematics lesson. What ideas from the lessons other group members shared are you interested in trying out in your classroom?
  - In Activity 10.3, you explored numerical reasoning strategies based on 10. What types of activities or lessons could you develop that would help students develop proficiency with this strategy?

References and Resources

Carpenter, T. P., Fennema, E., Franke, M. L., Levi, L., & Empson, S. B. (1999). *Children's mathematics: Cognitively guided instruction.* Portsmouth, NH: Heinemann.

Dolk, M., & Fosnot, C. T. (2006). *Fostering children's mathematical development: The landscape of learning* [CD-ROM]. Portsmouth, NH: Heinemann.

Fosnot, C. T., & Dolk, M. (2001). *Young mathematicians at work: Constructing number sense, addition, and subtraction.* Portsmouth, NH: Heinemann.

Fuson, K. C. (2004). Pre-K to Grade 2 goals and standards: Achieving 21st century mastery for all. In D. H. Clements, J. Sarama, & A.-M. DiBiase (Eds.), *Engaging young children in mathematics: Standards for early childhood mathematics education* (pp. 105–148). Mahwah, NJ: Lawrence Erlbaum.

Kilpatrick, J., Swafford, J., & Findell, B. (Eds.). (2001). *Adding it up: Helping children learn mathematics.* Washington, DC: National Academies Press.

Sarama, J., & Clements, D. H. (2009). *Early childhood mathematics education research: Learning trajectories for young children.* New York: Routledge.

Handout 10.2
Mathematics Games

Game of 10

Materials: One deck of playing cards with face cards removed

Groups: To be played in groups of two to four students

Purpose: To practice identifying combinations that make 10

- Place the stack of cards facedown on the table.
- The first player takes the top card and places it faceup.
- The next player turns over the next card from the stack.
- Players take turns placing cards until a 10 card is uncovered or until a card is uncovered that can be added to a previous card or cards to make 10.
- When players find a way to make 10 they demonstrate their discovery and take the cards they use. The unused cards remain and play continues until the stack is exhausted.
- The player with the most cards wins.

Sample:

| 3 | 6 | 5 | 2 |

Player 1 **Player 2** **Player 3** **Player 1**

Player 1 takes three cards and says "3 plus 5 plus 2 equals 10"

| 3 | 5 | 2 |

❖ ❖ ❖

Go Fish to Make 10

Materials: A deck of playing cards with the 10s and face cards removed

Groups: To be played in groups of two to four students

Purpose: Practice recognizing combinations that sum to 10

- Deal six cards to each player. Place the remaining cards in a draw pile facedown on the table.

- Player 1 begins by examining her hand for two-card combinations that sum to 10. (Note the ace represents 1.) If she has any, she states the numbers and lays these pairs down in front of her on the table. Each player in turn does the same.

- Now player 1 may ask a player for a card she needs to complete at 10. For example, "Mark, do you have a 6?" If Mark has a 6, he hands it to player one who states the combination of 10 and continues playing, asking other players for digits she needs. If Mark does not have a 6, he says, "go fish" and player 1 pulls a card from the draw pile and her turn is over.

- If at any time a player has no cards, he immediately draws from the pile.

- Play continues in this way until all the cards have been used.

- The player with the most 10 combinations is the winner.

Ten Concentration

Materials: A deck of playing cards with the 10s and face cards removed

Players: To be played in groups of two to four students.

Objective: Practice recognizing combinations that sum to 10

- Place cards face down in a six-by-six array.

- The object of the game is to find pairs of cards that sum to 10. (Note the ace represents 1.)

- Each player in turn completes the following:
  - Turns over two cards, and looks to see if the cards sum to 10.
  - If the cards sum to 10, the player claims both cards and turns over two more cards.
  - If the cards do not sum to 10, the player leaves the cards faceup and passes to the next player.
  - The next player turns over two new cards and may form sums of 10 with any faceup cards.
  - Players may claim more than one pair on each turn.

- The player with the most combinations is the winner.

Handout 10.4
Number Sense, Addition, and Subtraction Landscape of Learning

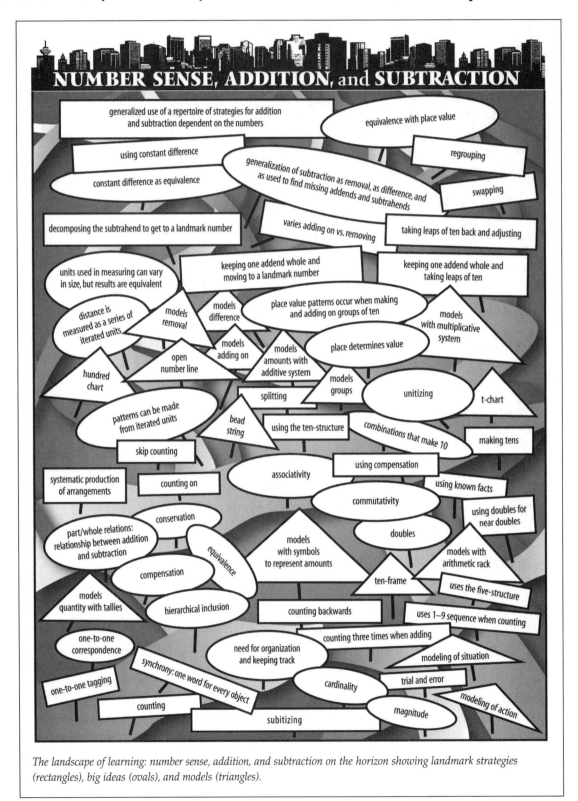

The landscape of learning: number sense, addition, and subtraction on the horizon showing landmark strategies (rectangles), big ideas (ovals), and models (triangles).

Handout 10.5
Student Connections: Observing Children Playing Games

Select at least one of the games from Handout 10.2 to play with three groups of children. Write notes here about the strategies students use to play the game.

Name of game	
Group 1	
Group 2	
Group 3	

Session 11

Mathematical Models Supporting Numerical Reasoning

Overview

How can mathematical models help students develop numerical reasoning strategies for addition and subtraction?

Description

Mathematical models can help students develop new concepts, make connections between concepts and between concepts and symbols, and communicate their thinking. Models can enhance students' ability to solve addition and subtraction problems and to develop stronger number sense.

Key Ideas

- The ability to translate concepts among different representations is an important component of students' mathematical development.

- In order to serve as a learning tool, a model must make sense to the student who is using it.

- The design of the prototype lesson is based on teachers' knowledge of student learning, content, and instruction.

- An understanding of the unit and how concepts develop within a unit is important when planning a lesson.

Outline of Activities

- 11.1 Mathematical Models   (25 minutes)
- 11.2 Prototype Lesson Template   (10 minutes)
- 11.3 Lesson Design: Three Themes   (25 minutes)
- 11.4 Mapping the Unit   (25 minutes)

What to Bring

- Handouts from previous sessions (4.4, 6.4, and 10.4)
- Notes and student work: Student Connections activities (Handouts 2.4, 3.5, 4.5, 5.5, 6.5, 8.5, and 10.5)
- Investigating Instructional Materials activities (Handouts 5.4A–E, 8.3A–E, and NCTM Illuminations activity with notes)
- Common Core State Standards: Standards for Mathematical Content

Facilitator Notes   Session 11

Mathematical Models Supporting Numerical Reasoning

If this is your first time facilitating the group, please refer to the more detailed facilitator guidelines in the Introduction. As the facilitator, it is generally your job to keep the conversation flowing and watch the clock. Use your judgment to decide when it's appropriate to extend a session for good conversation or when it's time to move on to the next activity. Remember to keep the group norms posted and revise them, as a group, as necessary.

Before the Session

- Make copies of the following handouts for each team member:
    - ☐ 11.1 Mathematical Models
    - ☐ 11.2 Prototype Lesson Overview
    - ☐ 11.4 Unit Map Template
- Gather the following materials to be used in this session:
    - ☐ Group norms (from Activity 1.4)
    - ☐ Unit plans or outlines (addition and subtraction) from different curricula, if available
    - ☐ Manipulatives
- Remind team members to bring the following items from previous sessions:
    - ☐ Journal (and writing instruments)
    - ☐ Handouts 4.4, 6.4, and 10.4
    - ☐ Notes and student work, Student Connections activities (Handouts 2.4, 3.5, 4.5, 5.5, 6.5, 8.5, and 10.5)
    - ☐ Investigating Instructional Materials activities (Handouts 5.4A–E, 8.3A–E, and NCTM Illuminations activity and notes)
    - ☐ Common Core State Standards: Standards for Mathematical Content

During the Session

- Post Group norms, and revise as a group as necessary.
- Activity 11.3: serve as recorder.

After the Session

- Pass any team materials to the next facilitator, including charted notes from Activity 11.3.

Activity 11.1 Mathematical Models

25 minutes

Handout 10.4 Landscape of Learning
Handout 11.1 Mathematical Models
Manipulatives (blocks, cubes, or counters)

A *mathematical model* is any picture, written symbol, oral language, real-world situation, or manipulative that can be used to represent a mathematical concept (Van de Walle, 2009). The use of manipulatives such as counters and blocks has become more widespread over the past few decades. These represent one type of model that can be very useful for helping children learn mathematics. However, there are many other models that can be used to build mathematical understanding. Number lines, ten frames, and hundreds grids are other models that help show relationships between numbers, operations, and number patterns.

Some teachers find that, given a choice, their students are more likely to use drawings, tally marks, and even their fingers than other types of commercially made manipulatives (Kamii, 2000). The most effective model will depend on the situation and the student. Sometimes it is helpful to select specific materials for students to use, as too many manipulative choices may impede the learning process. At other times, students can make their own choices about what models to use. A blank sheet of paper can be the best option—students can make their own models and they have an opportunity to decide the best strategy for organizing and representing their work.

Discuss how children would solve the following problem. What pictures, objects, or drawings might they use to work on a problem like this?

> Carol had 18 marbles. Her dad gave her 7 more marbles. How many marbles does she have now?

Review Handout 11.1 and examine the various mathematical models that could be used to solve this problem.

Discuss the following questions:

- Which of the models shown are ones that you have used with your students? Which are new to you?
- How are the models similar to or different from each other?
- Review the big ideas on the landscape of learning (Handout 10.4). How does each model support one or more of the big ideas on the landscape?

Solve the following problem using each of the models on the handout.

> Jake has 23 guppies. He gave 9 guppies to his cousin. How many guppies does he have left?

Discuss the following questions as you are working:

- How could each model build mathematical thinking?
- What are the potential limitations or disadvantages to each model?

Read these excerpts from Van de Walle (2004), *Elementary and Middle School Mathematics: Teaching Developmentally*:

To "see" in a model the concept that it represents, you must already have that concept—that relationship—in your mind. If you did not, then you would have no relationship to impose on the model. This is precisely why models are often more meaningful to the teacher than to students. The teacher already has the concept and can see it in the model. A student without the concept sees only the physical object. Mathematical concepts that children are in the process of constructing are not the well-informed ideas conceived by adults. New ideas are formulated little by little over time. As children actively reflect on their new ideas, they test them out through as many different avenues as we might provide. . . . Models give learners something to think about, explore with, talk about, and reason with. Three related uses for [models] in a developmental approach to teaching [include]:

> 1. To help children develop new concepts or relationships. 2. To help children make connections between concepts and symbols. 3. To assess children's understanding. (p. 30)

Reflect and write in your journals about the different models you examined during this activity.

- How do you react to the statement in the excerpt, "This is precisely why models are often more meaningful to the teacher than to students"? Have you found it to be true that students sometimes do not see the mathematics in the model?

- What strategies have you used or would you like to try to help ensure that students are working with models that make sense to them?

- Van de Walle suggests that models can help teachers assess children's understanding. Have you experienced this? How?

Share your ideas with others in your group.

Read and highlight the models on Handout 10.4, which are contained within the triangles on the landscape of learning.

Discuss the following:

- Compare the big ideas on the Dolk and Fosnot landscape with the models you included on your components of a learning landscape (Handout 2.3 in your journal). What similarities and differences can you identify? Is there anything your group would like to add to your components web?

- In your experience, which models are appropriate for use in kindergarten? Which models are appropriate for use in first grade? Which models are more appropriate in the second and third grades?

Activity 11.2 Prototype Lesson Template

10 minutes   Handout 11.2 Prototype Lesson: Overview

In Session 12, you will be using all the work you have done so far to develop a collaboratively designed prototype lesson. The purpose of the lesson is to put the knowledge and ideas you have generated into practice and to find out what the results are for students.

Read the following description of the prototype lesson.

The lesson you develop in this session of the *Teaching by Design* process is not intended to be perfect. Instead, the purpose is for you to have the experience of drawing on the group's shared expertise to craft a lesson that considers long- and short-term goals, important mathematical ideas, and appropriate instructional practices, all matched with the needs of students. The purpose also includes testing your ideas and hypotheses and revising based on what actually happens. This should lead to a new or deeper understanding. The prototype lesson is also an opportunity to gather data to address questions or hypotheses about student learning and to try out new ideas.

It is not necessary to start from scratch to design the prototype lesson. You may choose to start with an activity from your instructional materials or from the other instructional materials that you reviewed in previous sessions. Your team will add to this framework and adapt it so that you can enact the ideas related to the work you have been doing.

Review your copy of Handout 11.2 Prototype Lesson: Overview. It is intended to provide an overview of the content and format for designing a lesson. During the rest of this session, you will begin identifying ideas and questions that will inform the design of the prototype lesson. Keep the template in mind as you engage in the next two activities.

Activity 11.3 Lesson Design: Three Themes

25 minutes   Student Connections activities (Handouts 2.4, 3.5, 4.5, 5.5, 6.5, 8.5, and 10.5)

Handout 4.4 Common Core State Standards

Investigating Instructional Materials activities (Handouts 5.4A–E, and 8.3A–E)

Handout 6.4 Mathematical Proficiency

Handout 10.4 Landscape of Learning

Common Core State Standards: Standards for Mathematical Content

In this activity you will review your notes, handouts, and other materials from previous sessions. The purpose of this process is to identify the information and ideas that you have collected throughout the sessions. These ideas will guide the process of designing your prototype lesson in Session 12.

The broad content area of the prototype lesson will be number and operations. Based on the Common Core State Standards, which determined the topics covered in previous sessions, the lesson might focus on counting, comparing and ordering numbers, or addition and subtraction. The discussions in this activity are intended to help you hone in on the specific mathematical concepts for the prototype lesson.

Much of the information that you need for this activity will be captured in your Lesson Design Notes. However, the other handouts and materials may be helpful if you find that you need more information about a particular idea or question.

Gather and briefly review your Lesson Design Notes (Handout 1.3). Keep the other handouts and notes on hand for reference.

Scan the questions that follow and identify the ones that you believe have a high priority. You may not have time to discuss all of the questions in depth, so start with the questions that will help generate the most ideas. You should try to discuss questions related to all three *Teaching by Design* themes.

Discuss the questions and **record** your ideas on chart paper.

Where are we now?

- What do the results of the Student Connections activities tell us about our students?
- What are students' experiences with the number and operations concepts stated in the Common Core State Standards?
- What are students' strengths when it comes to these concepts?
- In what areas do students need support with these concepts?

Where do we want to go?

- What are our long-term goals for students?
- How are these goals related to the five strands of mathematical proficiency?
- How do your goals for students relate to the Common Core State Standards?
- Where do our students need to go next on the learning landscape?

What is the best way to get there?

- What mathematical concepts from the Common Core State Standards should our lesson address?
- What are the big ideas, strategies, and mathematical models associated with these concepts?
- What ideas from our investigations of instructional materials should we consider including in the lesson?

Informed by the ideas in your team's discussion, you will now select the mathematical concepts that will be addressed in your team's prototype lesson.

Identify the mathematical concept(s) that will serve as the focus of your team's prototype lesson and record it on the chart paper.

You will have additional opportunities to review your notes and discuss these questions as you plan the prototype lesson. Be sure to bring the chart paper notes to Session 12.

Activity 11.4 Mapping the Unit

25 minutes   Handout 11.4 Unit Map Template

In the previous activity, you identified the mathematics concepts that the prototype lesson will address. An understanding of how this lesson fits within a larger unit and how concepts develop within a unit is important when planning a lesson. Through the process of mapping or unit planning, you will gain a strong understanding of how each lesson fits with other lessons, and how skills and understanding of concepts develop.

Create an outline of the unit for the topic that you have identified. Handout 11.4 provides a template for this map of the unit. If your instructional materials include an outline in which the goals, mathematical concepts, and activities are described for each lesson, use this document as a starting point for the unit map.

It can be helpful to examine how different units on the same topic are sequenced in different curricula. If possible, compare your outline with other units that focus on the concepts for the unit you are mapping.

Discuss the following questions:

- How do your instructional materials address the topic you have selected?
- Which concepts does each lesson in the unit address?
- Are there sufficient opportunities for students to work on these ideas?
- Based on your work in previous sessions, do the lessons provide appropriate experiences that reflect how students learn?
- How are the lessons sequenced in the unit?
- What are the goals of the unit? What will students understand by the end of the unit?
- Which concepts are missing in the unit?

Revise the sequence of the unit as necessary. There may be changes that you identify in the flow of the lessons, such as revising the order in which certain strategies or concepts are presented. (This is an optional step that may not be necessary for the unit you have selected.)

Identify the lesson within the unit that you will collaboratively design as your team's prototype lesson. Consider the following questions in order to make your decision:

- Which lesson will have the most impact on the unit?
- Which lesson is the most challenging to teach?
- Why should we focus on this lesson?
- What will students learn in the activities leading up to the lesson?
- Where will they be going next?

In the next session, you will collaborate on designing the prototype lesson. Gather all the chart paper and other notes that you generated during this session. Be sure to bring all the relevant materials—see the overview page for Session 12 for a list.

References and Resources

Carpenter, T. P., Fennema, E., Franke, M. L., Levi, L., & Empson, S. B. (1999). *Children's mathematics: Cognitively guided instruction.* Portsmouth, NH: Heinemann.

Clement, L. (2004). A model for understanding, using, and connecting representations. *Teaching Children Mathematics, 11*(2), 97–102.

Fosnot, C. T., & Dolk, M. (2001). *Young mathematicians at work: Constructing number sense, addition, and subtraction.* Portsmouth, NH: Heinemann.

Fuson, K. C. (2004). Pre-K to Grade 2 goals and standards: Achieving 21st century mastery for all. In D. H. Clements, J. Sarama, & A.-M. DiBiase (Eds.), *Engaging young children in mathematics: Standards for early childhood mathematics education* (pp. 105–148). Mahwah, NJ: Lawrence Erlbaum.

Kamii, C. (with Houseman, L. B.). (2000). *Young children reinvent arithmetic: Implications of Piaget's theory* (2nd ed.). New York: Teachers College Press.

Kilpatrick, J., Swafford, J., & Findell, B. (Eds.). (2001). *Adding it up: Helping children learn mathematics.* Washington, DC: National Academies Press.

Van de Walle, J. A. (2004). *Elementary and middle school mathematics: Teaching developmentally* (5th ed.). Boston: Pearson Education.

Van de Walle, J. A. (2009). *Elementary and middle school mathematics: Teaching developmentally* (7th ed.). Needham Heights, MA: Allyn & Bacon.

Van den Heuvel-Panhuizen, M. (Ed.). (2001). *Children learn mathematics: A learning-teaching trajectory with intermediate attainment targets for calculation with whole numbers in primary school.* Rotterdam, the Netherlands: Sense Publishers.

Handout 11.1
Mathematical Models

Ten Frame

●	●
●	●
●	●
●	●
●	●

●	●
●	●
●	●
●	
●	

●	●
●	●
●	
●	
●	

Calendar

January						
Sunday	Monday	Tuesday	Wednesday	Thursday	Friday	Saturday
		1	2	3	4	5
6	7	8	9	10	11	12
13	14	15	16	17	18	19
20	21	22	23	24	25	26
27	28	29	30	31		

Number Line

0 1 2 3 4 5 6 7 8 9 10 11 12 13 14 15 16 17 18 19 20 21 22 23 24 25 26 27 28 29 30

1 to 100 Chart

1	2	3	4	5	6	7	8	9	10
11	12	13	14	15	16	17	18	19	20
21	22	23	24	25	26	27	28	29	30
31	32	33	34	35	36	37	38	39	40
41	42	43	44	45	46	47	48	49	50
51	52	53	54	55	56	57	58	59	60
61	62	63	64	65	66	67	68	69	70
71	72	73	74	75	76	77	78	79	80
81	82	83	84	85	86	87	88	89	90
91	92	93	94	95	96	97	98	99	100

Draw a Picture

(Make your own drawing in this space.)

Handout 11.2
Prototype Lesson: Overview

Design Team: [The team of teachers who designed the lesson]

Teacher: [The team member who teaches the prototype lesson]

School: **Grade Level:**

Title: [Descriptive name for the lesson]   **Date:**

Where are we now?

Background Information

[This section describes the research that the team conducted to design the prototype lesson and describes students' current understanding of the targeted mathematical concepts and skills.]

Where do we want to go?

[This section identifies the goals and outcomes that shape the details and design of the lesson.]

Unit Goals

[The broad goals of the unit in which the lesson occurs.]

Learning Outcomes

[The expected outcomes of the prototype lesson.]

Sequence of the Unit

[This section describes where the prototype lesson occurs in the unit, including the lessons that occur prior to the prototype lesson and those that occur after.]

Lesson 1	
Lesson 2	
Lesson 3	
Lesson 4	
Lesson 5	

Evaluation and Data Collection

[This section describes the specific data that will be collected during the teaching of the prototype lesson to determine the extent to which the goals and learning outcomes of the lesson were met.]

What is the best way to get there?

Lesson Outline

[This section describes the flow of the lesson in detail.]

Learning Activities and Teacher Questions	Expected Student Reactions	Teacher Support
[This column identifies what the students will be doing and how the teacher will set up and facilitate the tasks.]	[This column describes how the team anticipates students will respond to the tasks and teacher questions.]	[This column describes how the teacher will respond to the anticipated reactions from students.]

Handout 11.4
Unit Map Template

Title:

Title or Topic of the Lesson	Goal and Learning Activities

Session 12

Designing the Prototype Lesson

How can we use what we know about important mathematical concepts, student learning, and effective instructional elements to design a lesson?

Description

In this session, you will work collaboratively to develop the prototype lesson. Your group will use the ideas you have collected in your learning landscapes, what you have learned about your students, your understanding of the mathematical concepts from the Common Core State Standards, and your existing instructional materials to inform the design.

Key Ideas

- Teachers' research on pedagogy and student learning influences the design and content of a lesson.
- The purpose of creating a collaboratively designed prototype lesson is to improve instruction by generating professional knowledge, not by developing an exemplary lesson.

Outline of Activities

- 12.1 Overview of the Prototype Lesson Sessions
- 12.2 Background Information
- 12.3 Goals and Learning Outcomes
- 12.4 Evaluation and Data Collection
- 12.5 Lesson Process

Note: It is likely that it will take more than one session to design the lesson. Estimated times are not included for this session because the amount of time needed for the activities will vary.

What to Bring

- Handouts from previous sessions (4.4, 6.4, 10.4, and 11.4)
- Notes and student work: Student Connections activities (Handouts 2.4, 3.5, 4.5, 5.5, 6.5, 8.5, and 10.5)
- Investigating Instructional Materials activities (Handouts 5.4A–E, 8.3A–E, and NCTM Illuminations activity with notes)
- Common Core State Standards: Standards for Mathematical Content

To Complete Before Session 13

- Teach and observe the prototype lesson.

Facilitator Notes   Session 12

Designing the Prototype Lesson

If this is your first time facilitating the group, please refer to the more detailed facilitator guidelines in the Introduction. As the facilitator, it is generally your job to keep the conversation flowing and watch the clock. Use your judgment to decide when it's appropriate to extend a session for good conversation or when it's time to move on to the next activity. Remember to keep the group norms posted and revise them, as a group, as necessary.

Before the Session

- Make copies of the following handouts for each team member:
    - ☐ 12.2 Prototype Lesson: Template
- Gather the following materials to be used in this session:
    - ☐ Group norms (from Activity 1.4)
    - ☐ Charted notes (from Activity 11.3)
    - ☐ State mathematics standards or benchmarks
- Remind team members to bring the following items from previous sessions:
    - ☐ Journal (and writing instruments)
    - ☐ Handouts 4.4, 6.4, 10.4, and 11.4
    - ☐ Notes and student work, Student Connections activities (Handouts 2.4, 3.5, 4.5, 5.5, 6.5, 8.5, and 10.5)
    - ☐ Investigating Instructional Materials activities (Handouts 5.4A–E, 8.3A–E, and NCTM Illuminations activity and notes)
    - ☐ Common Core State Standards: Standards for Mathematical Content

During the Session

- Post group norms, and revise as a group as necessary.
- Activity 12.3: lead brainstorming, and serve as recorder of ideas.
- Next Steps activity: facilitate scheduling of lesson teaching.

After the Session

- Pass any team materials to the next facilitator.

Activity 12.1 Overview of the Prototype Lesson Sessions

The next three sessions will focus on designing, teaching, observing, discussing, and revising the prototype lesson. Before you start developing the lesson plan, it may be helpful to decide how you are going to collect information about the implementation of the lesson. Collecting data about student learning is an important step in determining the impact of the prototype lesson and in identifying ideas that can inform future lessons. You will be using the data to discuss the lesson in Session 13 and to revise the lesson in Session 14.

There are several different ways that teams of teachers can engage in this process:

Lesson study: One team member will volunteer to teach the lesson to her students and the other team members will observe the students. The team may choose to invite others to observe the lesson as well. The observers take detailed notes about what students do and say and report their findings back to the team. The advantage of having multiple observers is the ability to collect data on multiple groups of students.

Peer observation: Two teachers can pair up to observe the lesson in each other's classrooms. As in lesson study, the focus will be on collecting data on the students rather than observing the teacher.

Video study: Each team member will videotape the students as they engage in the lesson and review the tapes independently to observe student learning. It can be especially rich if each person identifies a brief segment to share with the whole group during the discussion of the prototype lesson.

Coaching: The coach will observe the lesson in the teachers' classrooms, focusing on students. It is also possible that the coach will teach the lesson and the teachers will observe. The coach and the teacher will share the data after the lesson.

If you will not be doing live observations or using video, it will be challenging to collect the data that you need for Sessions 13 and 14. If this is the only option, take as many notes as possible as you teach the lesson. Focus on a few students rather than trying to record everything that happens. It may be helpful to look at the discussion questions for Session 13 in order to identify the data that you will discuss. As soon as possible after the lesson, sit down and record as much as you can about what students said and did. In addition, analyze the student work. Identify the observations and examples that you want to share with the team in Session 13.

Discuss the options for collecting data and decide on the best strategy for your team.

Activity 12.2 Background Information

Student Connections activities (Handouts 2.4, 3.5, 4.5, 5.5, 6.5, 8.5, and 10.5)

Handout 4.4 Common Core State Standards

Handout 11.2 Prototype Lesson: Overview

Handout 11.4 Unit Map Template

Handout 12.2 Prototype Lesson: Template

Chart paper notes from Activity 11.3

Common Core State Standards: Standards for Mathematical Content

In this session, you will be using all the work you have done so far to develop a collaboratively designed prototype lesson using Handout 12.2 Prototype Lesson: Template. The notes that you have taken during previous sessions will serve as an important starting point for planning a lesson together. The materials listed are all resources that might be related to the goals and outcomes of the lesson. However, it is not necessary to consult all these notes and handouts, just the ones that are useful for your team.

Record the information for your design team, teacher, school, grade level, and date on Handout 12.2. You may find it helpful to refer to Handout 11.2 Prototype Lesson: Overview that includes a brief description of each section of the prototype lesson template.

The Background Information section of the lesson template provides a place to write about the research you did in preparation for designing the lesson. It is a place to make connections between the important mathematical concepts underlying the lesson and unit; the Common Core State Standards; the big ideas, strategies, and mathematical models in the learning landscape; your knowledge of student understanding; and your experience with instructional materials and strategies.

Develop and record the background information for the prototype lesson on Handout 12.2. To help you identify the information to include, you may want to consider the following questions. Select the questions that are most helpful or interesting to you—it is not necessary to answer all of them.

- Why was this lesson selected?
- How did you choose the learning activities in the lesson?
- Where does this lesson fall within the learning landscape?
- What Common Core State Standards are being addressed?
- What strand of mathematical proficiency is being addressed?
- Why is it important to have this lesson at this particular time in students' learning?
- What are the key instructional strategies needed for this lesson?
- What evidence of student learning will you collect?

Activity 12.3 Goals and Learning Outcomes

Handout 4.4 Common Core State Standards

Investigating Instructional Materials (Handouts 5.4A–E, and 8.3A–E)

Handout 6.4 Mathematical Proficiency

Handout 11.4 Unit Map Template

Chart paper notes from Activity 11.3

Common Core State Standards: Standards for Mathematical Content

Sequence of the Unit

The Sequence of the Unit section of the lesson plan template describes the instructional progression, including what students have learned prior to the prototype lesson and what their next steps will be. This section should refer to the unit map that you created in Session 11 (Handout 11.4).

Record the unit map in Sequence of the Unit on Handout 12.2. You can provide a summary in this section, or attach the handout to the lesson plan.

To get started on the lesson, you will identify goals and outcomes to shape the details and design of the lesson. You should consider both unit goals, which may have been developed in the unit planning phase—the overall goals for the unit within which the prototype lesson is located—and the lesson's expected outcomes for specific student learning.

Unit Goals

You may have identified or developed goals during Activity 11.4. Unit goals are usually broader than a lesson's expected outcomes and long-term in nature. For mathematics, there are sometimes two different types of unit goals. A content goal identifies the specific concepts or understandings. A process goal identifies the strategies, skills, or habits of mind that students will develop. You may find it helpful to refer to the five strands of mathematical proficiency (Handout 6.4) and the Common Core State Standards: Standards for Mathematical Practice (Handout 4.4) when identifying the process goals for the unit. Some examples of content and process goals are listed in the following table.

Unit Goals	
Content	Process
Children will develop flexible strategies for solving join and separate problems.	Children will effectively communicate their reasoning when solving a variety of join and separate problems.

Discuss the goals you have listed in your notes from Activity 11.4. Did you identify both content and process goals? How do these goals align with your state standards, Common Core State Standards, strands of mathematical proficiency, and learning landscape? What adaptations are needed to make the goals appropriate for the prototype lesson?

Record the goals for the unit on the Handout 12.2 Prototype Lesson: Template.

Learning Outcomes

The learning outcomes of your lesson should be directly related to the unit goals, but more specific. They serve as criteria for determining lesson effectiveness. The learning outcomes will help you decide what data to collect during the teaching of the lesson, as well as your discussion of the lesson after it has been taught (Session 13). Some examples of learning outcomes are listed in the following table.

Unit Goals		
Content	Process	Learning Outcomes
Children will develop flexible strategies for solving join and separate problems.	Children will effectively communicate their reasoning when solving a variety of join and separate problem types.	Children will identify and use appropriate strategies, such as direct modeling, counting, or numerical reasoning, to solve join and separate problems. Children will communicate their strategies to their peers and provide feedback to one another.

Brainstorm possible learning outcomes for the prototype lesson. Are these learning outcomes closely related to the goals of the unit? What skills and knowledge will be developed in this lesson?

Record the expected learning outcomes for the lesson on Handout 12.2 Prototype Lesson: Template.

Activity 12.4 Evaluation and Data Collection

The Evaluation and Data Collection section of the lesson template describes the specific data that will be collected when teaching the prototype lesson, and allows the team to determine the extent to which the goals and learning outcomes of the lesson were met. A key consideration in designing the prototype lesson is what you will have students doing so that learning is visible. The team should collect and review any written work produced by students during the lesson as well as any observer notes (what the teacher said, what students said and did) during their discussion and analysis of the lesson (Session 13). It is often helpful to have students work in pairs or small groups because the teacher and other observers can listen to student conversations. This is especially true when producing written work, which may be time-consuming and challenging for students.

Discuss what would convince the design team that the expected outcomes of the lesson were met.

- What kinds of data will help us assess students' progress toward the goals and learning outcomes?
- What work will students produce? What will this work tell us about student thinking?
- How will we check for understanding?
- What guiding questions will you provide observers to focus collection of data?

Record specific types of data that will be collected during the lesson in the Data Collection section of Handout 12.2. Data may include written student work, characteristics of student discussion, students' strategies, teacher questions, displays, and so on. Some examples of potential data sources are listed in the following box. It is a good idea to return to this section once you have finished designing the lesson to make sure that the data sources listed are appropriate and that your list is complete.

Data Collection

1. Observers will collect data.
   - What types of strategies did students use?
   - What confusion or misconceptions surfaced for students?
   - How are students using the manipulatives?
   - How are students keeping track of their solutions?

2. Student work will be collected and analyzed.
   - What does students' written work reveal about their understanding of the problem or areas of confusion?
   - How do students' drawings provide information about the strategies they used?

The Lesson Process section of the prototype lesson plan template describes the flow of the lesson in detail and includes three components:

- Learning activities and teacher questions
- Expected student responses
- Teacher support

Learning Activities and Teacher Questions

The first column outlines the learning activities and teacher questions—what students will be doing and how the teacher will set up and facilitate the tasks. This part of your lesson plan should be clear enough for someone who was not involved in the planning of the lesson to envision what will happen throughout the lesson. It is also often helpful to estimate how much time each phase of the lesson will take.

The learning activities and teacher questions column describes important points for the teacher to remember in setting up the learning activities, such as allowing time for student discussion. You should describe how the teacher and students will use the board or other visual aids during the lesson. The questions that the teacher will pose to students should be determined ahead of time and included in this section. As much as possible, consider the wording of the questions and prompts from the perspective of your students.

Develop and record the learning activities and teacher questions on Handout 12.2. The following questions may help you as you complete this column:

- How will the lesson be introduced?
- What activities follow?
- How will the lesson end?
- Does the flow of the lesson make sense?
- How will the goals and learning outcomes be made explicit for students?
- What are the main questions that students will explore?
- How will the activities be scaffolded to meet the needs of all students?
- What materials will be needed?

Example:

Learning Activities and Teacher Questions	Expected Student Responses	Teacher Support
Launch the problem: *Robbie has 9 comic books. His uncle gave him some more comic books. Now Robbie has 15 comic books. How many comic books did Robbie's uncle give him?*		

Expected Student Responses

The second column describes expected student responses to the learning activities and teacher questions. Consider the data that you have collected with the Student Connections activities, as well as the learning landscape, as you insert items into this column.

In order to generate possible student responses it is important to do the activities or tasks yourselves, keeping your students in mind. You may try out several different activities before you decide on the most effective one(s). Doing the activities in this way can also help you to identify potential difficulties that students may encounter with the content or learning activities. In addition, try to identify prior knowledge and potential misconceptions that the students will bring to the lesson.

Develop and record the expected student responses on Handout 12.2. Consider the range of students that you have in your class. The following questions may help you to complete this column:

- What will students think and do in response to each of the instructional activities?
- How might students respond to the questions?
- What strategies might students use?
- What answers might they give?
- When is it okay—or even desirable—for students to be confused?

Example:

Learning Activities and Teacher Questions	Expected Student Responses	Teacher Support
Launch the problem: *Robbie has 9 comic books. His uncle gave him some more comic books. Now Robbie has 15 comic books. How many comic books did Robbie's uncle give him?*	• Direct modeling strategy: Some children may use direct modeling and count out 9 objects. They may grab random numbers of cubes using guess and check until they have 15 altogether. • Some children may count out 9 objects, and then continue counting to 15 without keeping the objects in a separate pile. They may say 15 as an answer. • Counting strategy: Some children may say 9, and then while counting from 10 to 15, hold up one finger with each count. Then they will figure out how many fingers they're holding up to represent how many comics Robbie was given, and answer 6. • Some children may use the preceding counting strategy, but start counting with 9. Their answer would be 7. • Numerical reasoning: Some children may use numerical reasoning and say something like, "Since 10 plus 5 is 15, and 10 is one more than 9, I add 1 to the 5 to get 6. His uncle gave him 6 comics." • Some children may be confused and ask, "What do I do? Do I add 9 and 15? I don't understand what the problem is asking."	

Teacher Support

The third column—teacher support—describes how the teacher will respond to the anticipated responses from students. This includes questions that the teacher can pose to extend student thinking or to help students reevaluate their misconceptions. It can provide a contingency plan to enact if students struggle.

This section also provides thinking questions that the teacher can pose to students as they are working. You may want to list things to look for to identify the strategies that students are using or the ideas they are discussing. This will help the teacher to facilitate the closing of the lesson by identifying the students to call on or by anticipating how to bring new ideas into the discussion.

Develop and record your ideas for the Teacher Support section on Handout 12.2. The following questions may be of help as you complete this column.

- How can student misconceptions and confusion be addressed?
- What questions will further student understanding?
- What supports are necessary to provide access for all learners?
- How will the teacher help students who are struggling or frustrated?
- How will the teacher continue to challenge students who quickly finish the task?
- How can we rephrase the questions if students do not respond?
- How can we make the task more or less complex without undermining the goal?

Example:

Learning Activities and Teacher Questions	Expected Student Responses	Teacher Support
Launch the problem: *Robbie has 9 comic books. His uncle gave him some more comic books. Now Robbie has 15 comic books. How many comic books did Robbie's uncle give him?*	• Direct modeling strategy: Some children may use direct modeling and count out 9 objects. They may grab random numbers of cubes using guess and check until they have 15 altogether. • Some children may count out 9 objects, and then continue counting to 15 without keeping the objects in a separate pile. They may say 15 as an answer. • Counting strategy: Some children may say 9, and then while counting from 10 to 15, hold up one finger with each	As children are working, write down the strategies they use. Identify individuals who will share during the class discussion. Be sure to find a pair of students who are willing to share their struggles, as well as pairs that successfully solved the problem using methods further along the learning trajectory. As children are working, ask the following questions: • How were you thinking about this problem? • How did you solve it?

count. Then they will figure out how many fingers they're holding up to represent how many comics Robbie was given, and answer 6.

- Some children may use the preceding counting strategy, but start counting with 9. Their answer would be 7.

- Numerical reasoning: Some children may use numerical reasoning and say something like, "Since 10 plus 5 is 15, and 10 is one more than 9, I add 1 to the 5 to get 6. His uncle gave him 6 comics."

- Some children may be confused and ask, "What do I do? Do I add 9 and 15? I don't understand what the problem is asking."

- How can you record your strategy so that others can understand what you were thinking?

- How is your strategy similar to your classmate's strategy?

For students who finish before others and have recorded their approach in writing, provide another problem: *Robbie's big brother has 19 comic books. His uncle gave him some more comic books. Now his big brother has 25 comic books. How many comic books did Robbie's uncle give his brother?* Does the student see any relationship between this problem and the previous one?

For students who do not seem to understand what the problem is asking, prepare a picture with 9 comic books on a page. Then read the story. Show another picture with 15 comic books on the page. Does this provide enough concrete support to help the child identify an appropriate strategy to solving the problem? If this does not work, ask a child who uses direct modeling to show what he is doing and to make connections between the direct modeling and the action in the problem.

Next Steps

When the design of the prototype lesson is complete, the next step is to teach it in one or more classrooms and to gather data. The prototype lesson template will serve as the guide for teaching the lesson. It is important to stay as close as possible to the prototype plan. When you observe the lesson, either in the classroom or on video, you will use the plan to collect data.

If you are using observations in the classroom, it will be very important for the observers to stay focused on students rather than the teacher. Your data collection should include detailed notes about what students are doing and saying throughout the lesson. Observers should refer to the Evaluation and Data Collection section of the completed prototype lesson.

The next session will focus on discussing the results of the prototype lesson. The following artifacts will inform the discussion of the prototype lesson:

- Observation notes
- Video
- Student work
- Photos of any visual displays
- Teacher reflections

Handout 12.2
Prototype Lesson: Template

Design Team:

Teacher:

School: Grade Level:

Title: Date:

Where are we now?

Background Information

Where do we want to go?

Unit Goals

Learning Outcomes

Sequence of the Unit

Lesson 1	
Lesson 2	
Lesson 3	
Lesson 4	
Lesson 5	

Evaluation and Data Collection

1.

2.

3.

What is the best way to get there?

Lesson Outline

Learning Activities and Teacher Questions	Expected Student Responses	Teacher Support

Session **13**

Discussing Results

Overview

What does the evidence tell us about the impact of our lesson on student learning?

Description

The focus of this stage of the *Teaching by Design* process is on discussing the implementation of the prototype lesson and reviewing evidence about student learning. When engaging in a structured discussion process, the team identifies how students respond to each component of the lesson. This discussion serves as the basis for the lesson revision in Session 14.

Key Ideas

- Using multiple sources of data provides a reliable way to assess student learning.
- Collecting and examining data on student learning can inform teachers about the effectiveness of a lesson.

Outline of Activities

- 13.1 Reporting on the Lesson   (30 minutes)
- 13.2 Analyzing the Evidence   (60 minutes)
- 13.3 Review and Preview   (5 minutes)

What to Bring

- Copies of the prototype lesson
- Data collected during the teaching of the lesson, which might include students' written work, teachers' observation notes, teachers' reflections, video, photos of any visual displays

Facilitator Notes   Session 13

Discussing Results

If this is your first time facilitating the group, please refer to the more detailed facilitator guidelines in the Introduction. As the facilitator, it is generally your job to keep the conversation flowing and watch the clock. Use your judgment to decide when it's appropriate to extend a session for good conversation or when it's time to move on to the next activity. Remember to keep the group norms posted and revise them, as a group, as necessary.

Before the Session

- Make copies of the following handouts for each team member:
    - ☐ 13.2A Analyzing the Evidence: Data Sources
    - ☐ 13.2B Analyzing the Evidence: Learning Outcomes and Goals
- Gather the following materials to be used in this session:
    - ☐ Group norms (from Activity 1.4)
- Remind team members to bring the following items from previous sessions:
    - ☐ Journal (and writing instruments)
    - ☐ Handout 12.2
    - ☐ Copies of the prototype lesson
    - ☐ Data collected during the lesson

During the Session

- Post group norms, and revise as a group as necessary.
- Activity 13.1: help group adhere to guidelines.
- Activity 13.2: serve as recorder.

After the Session

- Pass any team materials on to the next facilitator.

Activity 13.1 Reporting on the Lesson

30 minutes

Copies of the prototype lesson

Notes from teaching or observing the lesson

Data collected while observing the lesson

In the time since your last session, one or more teachers from your team taught the *Teaching by Design* prototype lesson. In this session, you will describe what happened during the lesson and analyze the data collected during the teaching, with a focus on understanding how the lesson influenced student learning. Before you begin this process, review the group norms that were developed in Session 1.

The teacher (or teachers) who taught the lesson will provide an overview of what happened. It is important to observe the following guidelines during this process:

- There should be no interruptions from others.

- Listeners should write down any questions they have and ask them at the end of the teacher's presentation.

- Everyone in the group should have a copy of the lesson plan.

Teacher Report

The teacher(s) who taught the lesson should address the following questions (no more than 10 minutes):

- How did the lesson go?

- How did students respond to each part of the lesson?

- What components of the lesson plan were helpful while teaching?
  o Learning activities and teacher questions
  o Expected student responses
  o Teacher support

- Were there any surprises or unexpected student reactions?

- Were there any aspects of the lesson plan from which you deviated?
  o If so, how and why did you decide to deviate from the plan?
  o What were the results of this decision?

- Based on observations of student learning, what questions would you like the team to address in the next activity, after everyone has had a chance to share their observations?

If your team is using video study, each teacher may also show a clip during the discussion.

Observer Reports

If other team members were able to observe the lesson, they can now share highlights and important points from their notes (approximately 20 minutes). The emphasis in their comments should be on student learning and the implications of those comments for the design of the lesson. The purpose of the observer's report is not to evaluate or critique the teacher. If you are discussing more than one teaching and observation, consider the commonalities and differences between the episodes.

Observers discuss the following questions:

- What evidence of student learning did you see?

- Were there any surprises or unanticipated student responses? Misconceptions?

- Based on your observations related to student learning, what questions do you have about the lesson?

Activity 13.2 Analyzing the Evidence

60 minutes

Copies of the prototype lesson

Handout 13.2A Analyzing the Evidence: Data Sources

Handout 13.2B Analyzing the Evidence: Learning Outcomes and Goals

In this activity, you will be analyzing the evidence gathered during the teaching of the lesson as it relates to the goals and expected outcomes in the lesson. The discussion should include evidence collected from all of the classes in which the lesson was taught. If one group member taught the lesson while others observed, the evidence will be from one class. If the lesson was taught in multiple classes, the evidence from all of the classes will be examined (and additional time might be needed).

During this process, it is helpful to remember that the purpose of developing the prototype lesson in *Teaching by Design* is not to create a perfect lesson, but to have the experience of drawing on the group's shared expertise to craft a lesson that considers long- and short-term goals, important mathematical ideas, and appropriate instructional practices—all matched with the needs of students. This session will give you the opportunity to examine the evidence of student learning collected during the teaching and decide if students have met the goals of the lesson.

It is also helpful to remember that, as teachers, we sometimes are afraid of hurting the feelings of a group member and, as a result, comments and data analysis may only focus on the positive. It's important for teams to look closely at all of the evidence of student learning when deciding on the success of a lesson. The discussion should include both the strengths and weaknesses of the lesson based on the evidence of student learning.

It is important to note that certain mathematical concepts may take many lessons for students to build knowledge. An effective lesson does not always equate with all students accurately solving a given task with ease. A lesson can still be effective if students are building understanding of a concept.

Handouts 13.2A and 13.2B provide tools for capturing the results of this analysis. Your team should select the tool that seems the most useful, but if possible, use both handouts to conduct two cycles of analysis. Looking at the data from more than one perspective can reveal additional areas of success and needed improvement.

Review the handouts. Handout 13.2A is organized around the data sources that provide evidence about student learning. Handout 13.2B is organized around the learning outcomes for the lesson. You may decide to assign small groups to examine different pieces of data, or you may choose to all look at all of the data together. In either case, after investigating each source of data, discuss what it indicates about student learning and understanding. Use the handouts to record notes from your analyses and discussions.

List the data sources in the appropriate boxes on Handout 13.2A Analyzing the Evidence: Data Sources. You identified these sources in the plan for the prototype lesson. Be sure to include any additional sources of data as well.

Discuss and record your ideas about the following items in the appropriate boxes.

- Describe the data that was collected.
- What evidence is there of student understanding?
- What evidence is there of student misunderstanding?
- What is the evidence that the launch of the lesson provided adequate support for students to begin working on the problem(s)?
- What is the evidence that the lesson was adequately scaffolded for all students?

List the learning outcomes for the lesson in the appropriate boxes of the Learning Outcomes section on Handout 13.2B Analyzing the Evidence: Learning Outcomes and Goals.

Discuss and record your reactions to the following prompts in the appropriate boxes.

- What evidence is there that students met the expected outcomes of the lesson?
- What does the evidence tell you about how many achieved the learning outcomes? Can you tell how many students met the outcomes? How many students are close to achieving the outcomes? How many students still need a lot of work to meet the outcomes?
- Looking more closely at students who have met the outcomes, what evidence do you have about why they were successful?
- Looking more closely at students who are near meeting the outcomes, what evidence do you have to indicate what prevented them from meeting the outcomes? What types of instructional experiences might bring them closer to reaching the learning outcomes?
- Looking more closely at students who are still far from meeting the outcomes, what evidence do you have to indicate what prevented them from meeting the outcomes? What types of instructional experiences might bring them closer to reaching the learning outcomes?
- Were there any manipulatives, visuals, or organizers that might have helped or hindered students? What evidence supports this conclusion?
- How might you revise the design of the lesson to help students more effectively reach the learning outcomes? Record some ideas to use in the next session.

List the unit goals for the lesson in the appropriate boxes of the Unit Goals section on Handout 13.2B Analyzing the Evidence: Learning Outcomes and Goals.

Discuss and record your reactions to the following prompts in the appropriate boxes.

- What evidence is there that students have made progress toward the goals of the unit?
- What aspects of the lesson do you think contributed to students' progress toward the goals? What evidence supports this conclusion?

- What aspects of the lesson *did not* contribute to students' progress toward the unit goals? What evidence supports this conclusion?
- Based on the evidence of student learning discussed and the sequence of the unit, what would the next lesson in the unit look like? What would be the expected outcomes? What types of learning activities would you include? How would you meet the needs of students who show readiness for more challenging tasks? What supports would you provide to students who were struggling?

Activity 13.3 Review and Preview

5 minutes

Reviewing the Session

The key ideas for this session are

- Multiple sources of data are gathered and analyzed to assess student learning.
- Collecting and examining data on student learning can inform teachers of the effectiveness of a lesson.

Previewing the Next Session

In the next session, you will focus on revising the lesson and reflecting on your work. It will be the last session for the group, and your group will use the data from this session (Session 13) to revise your prototype lesson and reflect on what you learned from your work together.

Handout 13.2A

Analyzing the Evidence: Data Sources

Data Source:	
Evidence of Student Learning	Evidence of Misunderstanding

Data Source:	
Evidence of Student Learning	Evidence of Misunderstanding

Data Source:	
Evidence of Student Learning	Evidence of Misunderstanding

Handout 13.2B
Analyzing the Evidence: Learning Outcomes and Goals

Learning Outcomes

Learning Outcome:	
Evidence of Student Learning	Evidence of Misunderstanding

Learning Outcome:	
Evidence of Student Learning	Evidence of Misunderstanding

Unit Goals

Unit Goal:	
Evidence of Progress	Evidence of Lack of Progress

Unit Goal:	
Evidence of Progress	Evidence of Lack of Progress

Session 14

Reflecting On and Revising the Prototype Lesson

After analyzing the evidence of student learning and misunderstanding, what aspects of our prototype lesson plan will be revised?

Description

The final stage of the *Teaching by Design* process is revising the collaboratively designed prototype lesson, reflecting on the experience as a whole, and documenting your learning. This process is important because it enables the team to identify the ideas that will inform your mathematics teaching. It is also an opportunity to articulate and share professional knowledge.

Key Ideas

- Revising a lesson plan allows teachers to apply what they learned as a result of teaching the lesson and analyzing evidence of student understanding.
- Reflection is an essential part of professional learning.
- Capturing learning enables teachers to share professional knowledge with others.

Outline of Activities

- 14.1 Revising the Lesson   (60 minutes)
- 14.2 Final Reflections   (30 minutes)

What to Bring

- Copies of the prototype lesson
- Data collected during the teaching of the lesson, which might include students' written work, teachers' observation notes, teachers' reflections, video, and photos of any visual displays
- Handouts from previous sessions (13.2A and 13.2B)

Facilitator Notes   Session 14

Revising and Reflecting

If this is your first time facilitating the group, please refer to the more detailed facilitator guidelines in the Introduction. As the facilitator, it is generally your job to keep the conversation flowing and watch the clock. Use your judgment to decide when it's appropriate to extend a session for good conversation or when it's time to move on to the next activity. Remember to keep the group norms posted and revise them, as a group, as necessary.

Before the Session

- Make copies of the following handouts for each team member:
    - ☐ 14.1 Revising the Lesson
    - ☐ 14.2 *Teaching by Design* Reflection
- Gather the following materials to be used in this session:
    - ☐ Group norms (from Activity 1.4)
    - ☐ Chart paper
    - ☐ Markers
- Remind team members to bring the following items from previous sessions:
    - ☐ Journal (and writing instruments)
    - ☐ Copies of the prototype lesson
    - ☐ Data collected during the lesson
    - ☐ Handouts 13.2A and 13.2B

During the Session

- Post group norms, and revise as a group as necessary.
- Activity 14.1: help group navigate challenges, serve as recorder, and coordinate additional teaching or meetings.

After the Session

- Remind group of decisions to reteach or additional meetings scheduled.

Activity 14.1 Revising the Lesson

60 minutes
Handout 13.2A Analyzing the Evidence: Data Sources
Handout 13.2B Analyzing the Evidence: Learning Outcomes and Goals
Handout 14.1 Revising the Lesson
Copies of the prototype lesson
Data collected during the lesson

The purpose of developing the lesson in *Teaching by Design,* as explained in Session 12, is not to create a perfect lesson, but to have the experience of drawing on the group's shared expertise to craft a lesson that considers long- and short-term goals, important mathematical ideas, and appropriate instructional practices—all matched with the needs of students. This session will give you the opportunity to reflect on the degree to which your planning has been matched with the needs of the students and to make changes in your lesson so that you might better meet their needs in the future.

In the previous session, your group examined evidence of student learning from a variety of data sources. In this session, you will connect the evidence of student learning with the instructional activities in the lesson and make decisions about how to revise the lesson. Even a lesson that has gone well should be revised based on the data collected during the teaching of that lesson.

Identifying Components for Revision

Review Handouts 13.2A and 13.2B and any notes you took during Session 13. Look at the portions of the handouts that outline the evidence of student learning and misunderstanding.

Read Handout 14.1 and write your ideas on the chart. Your analysis and discussion from Session 13 should help you address the questions on the handout:

- What aspects of the lesson contributed to student learning and should remain in the lesson?
- How can the lesson be revised to more effectively help students achieve the expected outcomes and goals of the lesson?

Share your responses with the group and record the group's responses on chart paper.

Addressing Challenges in Revision

Groups may encounter a variety of challenges as they consider how to revise a lesson. Is your group struggling with any of the following?

Our group members can't agree on how to change the plan. Sometimes group members may have two or more different ideas for how to proceed. Sometimes the solution to this issue is to develop different versions of the lesson. If the revised lesson will be taught and observed, it may be helpful to leave the final decision up to the team member who will be teaching the lesson rather than developing multiple versions. Keep in mind that the revised version of the lesson, like any prototype lesson, is not set in stone. When teachers use the lesson in their classrooms, they will need to make adaptations to the plan.

Discuss how developing and teaching two different versions of the lesson plan might help or hinder the learning experience for the group. What are some drawbacks to having two different plans? Would group members feel safe to share the evidence of student learning for "their" plans?

Our lesson was horrible. We want to rewrite the whole thing. Sometimes a lesson does not go as planned. Improving the lesson often does not require a totally new plan. Consider making minor, but careful, revisions before teaching it again. Perhaps the group miscalculated students' prior knowledge and skills or the task did not motivate students. This is a great learning opportunity. Again, the purpose of developing the prototype lesson in *Teaching by Design* is not to create a perfect lesson, but to have the experience of drawing on the group's shared expertise to craft a lesson that considers long- and short-term goals, important mathematical ideas, and appropriate instructional practices—all matched with the needs of students.

Discuss areas of the lesson where there is evidence of student learning. You might consider keeping these aspects of the lesson. Where did students struggle? How might the task be reworked, questions rephrased, the use of manipulatives either included or removed, or visual materials adapted to better help students achieve the goals of the lesson?

The lesson is too hard. Many students didn't get it. We need to make the lesson easier. Often in this type of professional learning experience, we err on the side of developing a lesson where all students experience immediate success. As a result, the lesson loses its rigor and fails to address important mathematical concepts. In other cases, we develop lessons which are so challenging that no students can reach the goals we have for them. This may be because we have not considered the necessary prerequisite knowledge and skills students need to accomplish the tasks we assign, or because we have expected them to learn too much too quickly. In these cases, it is important to consider whether the confusion students experience will help them learn in the long run, or whether it will interfere with their learning in the future. There may be occasions when it is desirable for students to experience confusion and a sense of disequilibrium. The lesson will never be perfect. What did not work informs what you will do the next day—consolidation of learning is important. The key is that you are not only aware of potential challenges or difficult concepts, but also have planned for them by identifying broad unit goals and what each lesson in the unit will address.

Discuss when it may be desirable for students to be confused and experience disequilibrium. What are the benefits of confusion? What are some of the challenges in having students work past their confusion?

The lesson was great! We don't need to make any changes. Sometimes all students are on task during a lesson, and it may appear that there aren't any changes that need to be made. Other times, comments and data analysis may only focus on the positive, for fear of hurting the group member's feelings if any questions are raised about the lesson. It's important for teams to look closely at all of the evidence of student learning when deciding on the success of a lesson.

Discuss whether or not all of the students showed evidence of learning. How might students be further challenged? Was the lesson rigorous enough? Are there additional supports that might be added for students with special needs?

Making Lesson Changes

Review what the group listed on the chart paper and Handout 14.1. Discuss and decide on the changes you will make in the revised version of the lesson.

Documenting Changes

You and your group are now ready to document changes to your lesson plan. It is important to keep a copy of your original plan. If you are using a computer, be sure to save the revised lesson as another document file. It is also important to be able to compare the first and second versions of the lesson. This comparison can take place when the team discusses the results of the reteaching.

Reteaching the Lesson

You and your group members will probably want to teach the revised lesson in a class that did not experience the first version. Benefits to teaching the revised lesson include the following characteristics:

- The revised lesson uses classroom data to inform the development of the lesson.
- Another opportunity to teach or observe the lesson provides you with another learning experience.
- Revising and reteaching the lesson allows your group to investigate different ideas of mathematics instruction.
- Collecting evidence of student learning from the teaching of the second lesson will allow you to make comparisons between the differences in impact on student learning between the two lesson plans.

Discuss whether or not your group will teach the revised lesson. What would you gain from teaching the revised lesson? When could you find time to discuss the results of the revised lesson?

Activity 14.2 Final Reflections

30 minutes   Handout 14.2 *Teaching by Design* Reflection
                              All handouts, journal entries, and notes from all previous sessions

The process of reflecting on professional development is a key step in ensuring that your experiences lead to learning and change. Reflection enables you to extract knowledge from experiences and frame questions about the assumptions that influence your teaching. Reflection also allows you to identify areas of strength in your knowledge about students, instruction, and mathematics, as well as areas where more learning would be helpful. Reflection is a key to formulating the next steps in your professional growth.

Review the expected outcomes described at the beginning of this volume and reproduced as follows.

Expected Outcomes for Teaching by Design in Elementary Mathematics

- Teachers will deepen their content knowledge for important mathematical concepts in their grade.
- Teachers will increase their understanding of how students learn these mathematical ideas.
- Teachers will use their knowledge to develop effective lessons and improve instruction.
- Teachers will enhance their collaboration skills.

Collect your thoughts about these outcomes on Handout 14.2.

Record your reactions to the following questions in your journal:

- In what ways did you deepen your content knowledge for number and operation concepts described in the Common Core State Standards for kindergarten and first grade?
- What did you learn about how students learn these mathematical ideas?
- How did you use this knowledge in the development of a lesson plan?
- In what ways did you enhance your collaboration with your colleagues?

References and Resources

Stepanek, J., Appel, G., Leong, M., Mangan, M. T., Mitchell, M. (2007). *Leading lesson study: A practical guide for teachers and facilitators.* Thousand Oaks, CA: Corwin.

Handout 14.1
Revising the Lesson

What aspects of the lesson contributed to student learning and should remain in the lesson?	How can the lesson be revised to more effectively help students achieve the expected outcomes and goals of the lesson?

Handout 14.2
Teaching by Design Reflection

To what extent did you achieve the expected outcomes for *Teaching by Design in Elementary Mathematics?*

- Teachers will deepen their content knowledge for important mathematical concepts in their grade.

- Teachers will increase their understanding of how students learn these mathematical ideas.

- Teachers will use their knowledge to develop effective lessons and improve instruction.

- Teachers will enhance their collaboration skills.

Successes: What worked? What helped produce positive outcomes?

Challenges: What didn't work? In hindsight, what would I/we have changed?

Next steps: Do we want to continue? What should we focus on next?

Index

CORWIN

A SAGE Company

The Corwin logo—a raven striding across an open book—represents the union of courage and learning. Corwin is committed to improving education for all learners by publishing books and other professionaldevelopment resources for those serving the field of PreK–12 education. By providing practical, hands-on materials, Corwin continues to carry out the promise of its motto: **"Helping Educators Do Their Work Better."**

CREATING STRONG
SCHOOLS & COMMUNITIES

Education Northwest, formerly known as the Northwest Regional Educational Laboratory, is a nonprofit organization dedicated to transforming teaching and learning. We work with educators, administrators, policymakers, and communities across the country. Headquartered in Portland, Oregon, our mission is to improve learning by building capacity in schools, families, and communities through applied research and development. More information about Education Northwest is available at educationnorthwest.org.